MEGAQUAKE

MEGAQUAKE

How Japan and the
World Should Respond

Tetsuo Takashima

Translated and edited by Robert D. Eldridge

POTOMAC BOOKS
An imprint of the University of Nebraska Press

© 2015 by Robert D. Eldridge and Tetsuo Takashima
Originally published by Shueisha Inc. as *Kyodai
Jishin no Hi Inochi o Mamoru Tame no Hontō
no Koto* © 2006 by Tetsuo Takashima

All rights reserved. Potomac Books is an
imprint of the University of Nebraska Press.
Manufactured in the United States of America.

Library of Congress Cataloging-in-Publication Data
Takashima, Tetsuo, 1949–
[Kyodai jishin no hi. English]
Megaquake: how Japan and the world should
respond / Tetsuo Takashima; translated
and edited by Robert D. Eldridge.
pages   cm
Translation of the author's Kyodai jishin no hi.
Includes bibliographical references and index.
ISBN 978-1-61234-664-9 (cloth: alk. paper)
ISBN 978-1-61234-665-6 (pdf)
1. Disaster management—Japan.
2. Earthquakes—Japan. 3. Natural disasters—
Japan. 4. Economic assistance—Japan.
5. Technical assistance—Japan. I. Title.
HV551.5.J3T35 2014
363.34'9560952—dc23
2014037022

Set in Charis by Lindsey Auten.
Designed by N. Putens.

Contents

Translator's Foreword

I first met the author, Takashima Tetsuo, in May 2007. He and I were speakers in a course taught at the Osaka University School of International Public Policy (Ōsaka Daigaku Kokusai Kōkyō Seisaku Kenkyūka). I had co-founded the course in the fall of 2001 with a colleague, Professor Hoshino Toshiya, and Maj. Gen. Kasahara Naoki of the Japanese Ground Self-Defense Force, or GSDF (Rikujō Jieitai), the then director of the Osaka Provincial Liaison Office (Ōsaka Chihō Renraku Honbu), which represents the interests of all three services making up the Self-Defense Forces, or SDF (Jieitai) in Osaka Prefecture.[1] I did not know of Takashima at that point, other than the fact that his novel, *Midonaito iiguru* (Midnight eagle)— about the race to secure a tactical nuclear weapon that was loaded on a Japan-based American stealth bomber that had crashed in the Japan Alps in winter—had been turned into a movie earlier that year. Since one of the main characters in the movie was a soldier in the GSDF, my SDF counterparts, who arranged to invite Takashima to the class, were particularly excited to welcome him.

The purpose of the pioneer course, known as the Workshop on International Security, or WINS (Kokusai Anzen Hōshō Waakush-oppu), was to have leading experts, government officials, and military officers brief and discuss aspects of international or regional security issues with graduate students and SDF personnel attending the graduate program of the National Defense Academy (Bōei Daigakkō).[2] The course included a series of on-site visits—to a nuclear reactor in Fukui Prefecture, the Disaster Reduction Museum (Hito to Mirai Bōsai Sentaa) in Kobe, and various SDF bases and facilities—and it concluded with a two- to three-day retreat to Camp Itami for all-day and all-night discussions leading up to a presentation based on a certain scenario that often changed or evolved rapidly in order to challenge the students (and to reflect real-world, real-time situations). Beginning in 2005, following the earthquake and tsunami in Indonesia and South and Southeast Asia, we began looking more and more at natural disasters, particularly domestic ones in Japan. It was for this reason in particular that Takashima was invited.

Takashima has had an interesting career. He was born in 1949 in Okayama Prefecture, between Kobe and Hiroshima. He still lives not too far from Okayama, in Tarumi Ward, Kobe, in the very western part of Japan's fifth-largest city. After studying in the Engineering Department of Keio University in Tokyo, he began working as a researcher for the Japan Atomic Energy Research Institute (Nihon Genshiryoku Kenkyū Kaihatsu Kikō), created in 1956. Subsequently he moved to the United States, where he conducted further studies at the University of California. Upon his return to Japan he began writing while managing a private preparatory school. *Merutodaun* (*Fallout: A Novel*) was his debut novel and won the 1994 Shōsetsu Gendai Mystery Newcomer Award. Other novels include the action thriller *Intruder*, which won the 1999 Suntory Mystery Award. Takashima has written more than twenty novels in the action, thriller, suspense, mystery, and juvenile fiction genres. His most recent book, among many other projects, is a novel titled *Shuto hōkai* (Collapse of the capital), on the worldwide economic consequences of an earthquake in Tokyo.

One of the many books Takashima has published is *Kyodai jishin no hi: Inochi o mamoru tame no hontō no koto* (The day the large-scale earthquake comes to Japan: What we all truly need to know to preserve life), which is the original version of the translation you have in your hands and which I have chosen to title *Megaquake*.[3] Unlike most of Takashima's books, this one is not a novel, not fiction. It is frighteningly real and is in part based on both extensive research and his own experiences in the Great Hanshin-Awaji Earthquake (which I also experienced as a first-year graduate student at the Kobe University Graduate School of Law [Kōbe Daigaku Daigakuin Hōgaku Kenkyūka]). That book was published in March 2006, five years before a big earthquake—a true megaquake—and tsunami struck the Pacific coast off of northeast Japan. That magnitude 9.0 (M9) earthquake is known as the Great East Japan Earthquake and Tsunami (Higashi Nihon Daishinsai).

It was shortly after I returned from serving as the political adviser to the Forward Command Element of the Marine Expeditionary Brigade, which became the headquarters for forward-deployed U.S. Forces Japan in Sendai, Miyagi Prefecture—the heart of the disaster area—that I contacted Takashima, with whom I had not been in touch for some time.[4] I urged him to consider an English-language version of his book, knowing that future disasters were very likely and believing that it was necessary to share the insights of this prolific and perceptive writer. I volunteered to be the translator.

I am not sure if Takashima was expecting to hear from me. We had not exactly hit it off when he visited my class four years before. For my part of the class I introduced the policy recommendations on the use of U.S. forces in Japan in the event of a large-scale natural disaster—essentially the formula by which we responded to the March 11 disaster; I co-wrote these recommendations in a study with Maj. Alfred J. Woodfin, a U.S. Marine foreign area officer who had been studying in Japan and was affiliated with Osaka University's Center for International Security Studies and Policy (Kokusai Anzen Hoshō Seisaku Kenkyū Sentaa).[5] Takashima seemed to listen to my presentation with some concern or discomfort, a body language I had sensed from other people in the past who seemed to doubt the need for U.S. forces to be involved. At the minimum he did not openly embrace my recommendations.

The origin of that study and set of policy recommendations, including the signing of a mutual assistance agreement in natural disasters—in which the SDF would deploy to the United States or its islands, including Guam, Saipan, and Hawaii, for humanitarian assistance and disaster relief—was based on a conference I organized at Osaka University in January 2006 entitled "One Year after the Tsunami." The conference brought together a diverse group of military officers, government officials, non-government organizations (NGOs), non-profit organizations (NPOs), and academics from a half dozen countries connected to or interested in the response to the earthquake and tsunami that struck South and Southeast Asia in December 2004 and killed more than 220,000 people.[6] While much of the discussion focused on Japan's proactive and fairly quick response to the tragedy in Indonesia, Thailand, Sri Lanka, and other parts of the region, during none of the comments that day did a speaker, panelist, commentator, or member of the audience ask what would happen if the situation were reversed. In other words, what would happen if a similar event occurred in Japan? Was Japan prepared to accept international aid amid a massive disaster?

Having experienced the Kobe earthquake, when Japan turned away most offers of international help; having served as a volunteer and later as a volunteer interpreter for a U.S. aid organization (AmeriCares); and having seen firsthand the Japanese bureaucracy paralyzed and resistant to outside help, I wondered if Japan had truly learned any lessons in the interim or fundamentally made any changes. While there had been some improvements at the superficial level, unfortunately I found my concerns to be justified after I conducted the study with Major Woodfin. We published the study not only in English in March 2006 (the same time, coincidentally, that Takashima's book came out), but in Japanese as well later that year and widely disseminated it to Japanese and American government officials and military officers.[7]

During the research I was disappointed to discover that not only had Japanese officials not really thought about the issue of international aid, and especially the role of U.S. personnel who already lived and worked in Japan, but also few Japanese people—whether they were government officials, SDF members, disaster experts, politicians, or scholars—seemed willing to entertain the idea of utilizing U.S. forward-deployed troops and equipment. Even after we conducted the detailed research and wrote up the policy recommendations and presented them, we continued to face resistance to the idea of utilizing U.S. forces in Japan in large-scale disasters or utilizing the SDF in natural or other disasters in the United States. The Japanese bureaucracy and military were unwilling to consider such possibilities, and Japan's political leaders seemed unaware of the need to pursue them.

Equally disturbing were the trends I saw in Japanese officials underestimating the scale of the destruction in different scenarios (trends you will see in some of the official figures cited in this book by Takashima—which, to his credit, he challenges). These figures were already artificially (and purposely) low but were even more ridiculous in light of the March 11, 2011, Great East Japan Earthquake and Tsunami, which killed and left missing close to twenty thousand people. Because of the artificially low destruction estimates, Japanese elected leaders and bureaucrats had tragically overestimated their ability to respond to crises in Japan and thus had challenged the idea of accepting international support other than for symbolic reasons such as goodwill and friendship.

Surprisingly some American audiences also doubted the need for U.S. support to Japan in a large-scale disaster. Following my presentation at a bilateral workshop in Washington DC, co-organized with the Institute for Foreign Policy Analysis in December 2006, an official from the U.S. Agency for International Development (USAID) brushed off my concerns, saying, "Japan is a modern country and can handle such a situation on its own."[8] Not able to accept his indifference to the issue, particularly as I myself live in Japan and would have been at the mercy of the Japanese government's decision making, I challenged his view with some passion, and a "frank" discussion ensued.[9]

Needless to say, it was very apparent in the minutes following the March 11 disaster that American help was going to be necessary, and I whipped out my set of recommendations as we began planning and implementing our response. (By chance, I had shared the study and set of recommendations with a friend who worked in the Cabinet Office on March 10, the day before the earthquake, to help the then prime minister, Kan Naoto, prepare for a planned May (2011) meeting with U.S. president Barack H. Obama. I had shared them with the Okinawa Prefecture government as well prior to the disaster in order to facilitate discussions on local partnering.)

As hinted above, when we first met, I felt Takashima was one of those who doubted the likely need to use U.S. forces in Japan. In chapter 4 of this book, for example, he mentions the U.S. offer to provide support after the Kobe earthquake, notes the Japanese reluctance to accept it, and seems understanding or accepting of that reluctance.

I know Takashima has since come to better understand the important role U.S. forces played in the interim. Symbolic of this new understanding, during a talk he gave in May 2014 before marines and sailors at the headquarters building of III Marine Expeditionary Force (MEF) in Okinawa, Takashima played a video introducing Japanese citizens from the Tohoku disaster thanking U.S. forces for their support following the March 11 disaster. In our correspondence after the earthquake, he noted that "the people of Japan have been given courage thanks to the help of the United States and other nations,"[10] and he makes a similar point in the epilogue. Indeed as my boss, Lt. Gen. Kenneth J. Glueck Jr., commanding general of the III MEF at the time, has repeatedly said, "The greatest thing that U.S. forces [which provided twenty thousand military personnel to the U.S. effort to assist Japan in what is known as "Operation Tomodachi"] gave to the people of Japan was a sense of hope."[11]

There was one thing Takashima and I clearly agreed on: the Great East Japan Earthquake and Tsunami was just the beginning of more disasters to come, and it was important to prepare now, ahead of time. In the same exchange noted above, he wrote, "This is not the end but the beginning. We must prepare for the future."[12] Yes, indeed. It was for this reason especially, and another one introduced below, that I felt it was important to translate Takashima's book and share it with a wider, non-Japanese-speaking audience in Japan and around the world.

The first reason, as mentioned, is that Japan will definitely experience another tragic disaster, another megaquake, in the near future. The question is not if but when, and it will probably be far worse than what happened off the relatively sparsely populated coasts of northeast Japan. I believe the disaster that struck the Tohoku region was a warning that we need to prepare for an even bigger one. That next disaster will certainly go well beyond Japan's capabilities, especially those of its SDF, to respond quickly and effectively. This is not a criticism of Japan—no country on its own can, or should have to, deal with a megaquake and tsunami and all of the additional complications by itself. We are in this together—not only Japan's only formal ally, the United States, but everyone in the region and/or everyone who has relations with Japan. As Takashima writes in the preface to the English edition, "We are all interconnected." Japan will certainly need the international community's help, and the international community will need to know Japan's situation then, if not now, so that it can better respond and assist. In addition, as Takashima's recent work about the worldwide economic consequences of a major disaster in the nation's commercial, political, and governmental capital highlights, international society is very much interconnected.

Second, there are lessons for every society to be found in this book, no matter what the disaster. Ironically as our cities and communities become more modern, we also become more fragile and vulnerable. Takashima brilliantly lays out the challenges when a society is facing an earthquake and tsunami, but the lessons apply to other types of disasters, particularly as they turn into complex emergencies (such as with the nuclear reactor problem at Fukushima) or secondary effects (such as health, sanitation, disease, and other medical issues or a collapse into civil unrest [not likely but not impossible]). Indeed the third-order effects of national, regional, and international economic collapse cannot be ignored either; these will have social, diplomatic, and even military implications. As some readers know and as Takashima discusses in chapter 2, panic and unrest led to vigilantism after the 1923 Great Kanto Earthquake, and thousands of innocent people (many residents of Korean descent in Japan) were murdered, increasing the human toll of the disaster.[13] Geologically speaking, some scientists are even detecting disturbing patterns of major volcanic activity following megaquakes, and attention is being given to a Mount Fuji eruption following a major quake in Japan.

When I was working in Sendai in March 2011, amid the massive and heart-wrenching devastation and countless frightening aftershocks, I could not help but think that it was a warning to us that this was just the beginning. Japan, which experiences some 23 percent of the world's earthquakes over magnitude 6 on the Richter Scale, will likely see another earthquake and tsunami in the following areas: in Tokyo (one of the world's largest cities with approximately a fifth of the population of Japan in it or its immediate vicinity); southwest of Tokyo (centered near Shizuoka Prefecture and known as the Tokai, or East Seas, earthquake scenario); further south along the Pacific coast past Nagoya City, all the way to the Kii Peninsula (known as the Tonankai, or Southeast Seas, earthquake scenario); off of Shikoku Island, with a half-dozen prefectures affected, including Osaka (called the Nankai, or South Seas, earthquake scenario); or elsewhere in the far south or far north of Japan or along faults with which we are unfamiliar or have doubted the probability of something happening along them (like what happened in the 1995 earthquake in Kobe).

Takashima published this book with the general reader in mind. He has taken scientific and academic studies (removing some of the jargon), as well as government reports, and introduced the essence of the debates, arguments, controversies, issues, and contents to educate readers on what to expect and what to prepare for in a massive earthquake and tsunami. Unfortunately Takashima was only too prophetic; almost five years to the day after publication of the book in Japanese (and the issue of my co-authored report as well), a megaquake and tsunami did indeed strike northeastern Japan. My hope as translator for this book is that English-language readers—men and women from the military, government, NGOs, NPOs, international organizations, academia, and the media; scientists, students, volunteers, and foreign residents—will make the most of the lessons that Japan, which has experienced a significant number of natural disasters, has to teach us. We owe Takashima our gratitude for this book and his other writings and efforts.

This book was originally meant to sound a warning; the English version is building on Takashima's effort to now transmit that warning to a wider, international audience. In chapter 4 Takashima cites an engraving on a monument built in 1855 in Osaka on the site of earlier earthquakes and tsunamis: "Pray for the souls of the victims; this is a poorly written message but it will be recorded here; I pray that a caring person will put ink into the engraving as time goes on to make it more legible and let this story be told." This is essentially what this book, in both the Japanese original version and the English translation, is trying to do—retell and add to the stories of dealing with disasters.

I have told audiences over the past several years that I was working on this translation and, more important, why I was doing so.[14] Originally, as noted, I had two reasons in mind when I suggested it to Takashima, but the more I worked on this project, spoke with people in the various aforementioned settings, and interviewed Takashima more, the reasons—or I should say the significance—of the translation grew in my eyes as well as the eyes of the people and experts with whom I met.

As noted, based on the high likelihood that another, and perhaps larger and more deadly, disaster is awaiting Japan that will go beyond the capabilities of the Japan SDF and the larger government of Japan singularly to respond, international support—even much greater than we saw during Operation Tomodachi—will be necessary. This book is meant to provide insights into the state of Japan's preparations, where it is weak and where it is probably "good to go," so that international assistance can be more timely, efficient, and effective. It is, in other words, to serve as a basic manual or guide for understanding Japan's disaster readiness.

One of the biggest lessons learned by Japanese and U.S. forces in Operation Tomodachi was the recognition of the need to be able to work together and the lack of knowledge, especially by the Japanese side, of U.S. military capabilities.[15] I pointed out these concerns five years before the disaster in "Planning for the Inevitable" and called on the two countries to work together more in this area, formalizing the relationship at the national level with a mutual disaster assistance agreement. Unfortunately it took the March 11 disaster to get the two sides to begin to deepen that relationship.

We still have a long way to go. Little has changed at the action level, despite efforts by the U.S. side, particularly the Marine Corps. The SDF, particularly the GSDF, still has much to do in enhancing cooperation with the United States. An after-action review (AAR) conference sponsored by the Ground Staff Office (Rikubaku) on March 8, 2012, at Camp Ichigaya (which I attended as an observer) identified several problems but missed (in my opinion) many more.[16] That is to be expected: no one person, no one organization, no one country, has all the answers. This is why cooperation among people, organizations, and nations is so important.

My desire in particular now is to continue to promote the ability of local communities and U.S. military forces in Japan to work together seamlessly in the case of a natural disaster in Japan because in any of the scenarios described in Takashima's book for an earthquake and tsunami, it will highly likely be beyond the capabilities of the SDF to respond quickly or fully. U.S. forces may be the first ones—or only ones—on the scene. It will be important for local communities to know more about the capabilities of the U.S. military, and vice-versa, and how to work together, just like it was for the SDF and U.S. military in March 2011. It would be a shame if this issue—"local communities and U.S. personnel need to know each other better"— were identified in someone's AAR as a lesson learned in the future after the *next* disaster. For this reason, too, I wanted to see the book published in English so that the international community, especially U.S. forces in Japan, would have a better idea of how to assist this earthquake and tsunami-prone country. Because leaders and personnel in the military and officials in the government rotate quite regularly, it is important to keep the memory and lessons alive. In addition, as noted, it is my hope that the wider international community will learn from this book and apply some of its lessons and information, as appropriate.

In doing this translation, I rediscovered the fact that there is a true dearth of information available in English about Japan's preparations, experiences, and lessons learned after each disaster. I have long urged Japanese government officials to get their reports and recommendations published in foreign languages, especially English, and to regularly brief foreign embassies and consular offices both in Tokyo and in other areas on the latest estimates and response planning. As the epilogue for the English edition (written exclusively for this book) shows, some reports are finally being made available in

English. However, it takes time, and thus I wanted to get this book out as quickly as possible.

A follow-on but not necessarily less important reason for the information in this book to be widely shared was pointed out by Takashima in a conversation I had with him. It had to do with global and especially economic interdependence. He laid out the economic impact that a major disaster in the Tokyo area would have or the disaster a Tokai, Tonankai, or Nankai earthquake would bring about. Not only in area of finance, but also those of commerce and trade, in which Japan, as the third largest economic power, is a key player, would be greatly affected. This interdependence was made clear in the recent Tohoku disaster, where many of Japan's factories are located, and in the flooding in Thailand, where the factors of Japan and other nations are also located. Production stopped, causing other assembly plants in other parts of the world to slow down or shut down. The ripple effects were large and immediate. In a worst-case situation, Japan might have to sell its U.S. bonds, for which it is the second-largest holder, in order to pay for the rebuilding and recovery. China, Korea, Southeast Asia, South Asia, the Middle East, Europe, and Africa would all feel the effects. Although Japan's economic and political influence has declined significantly over the past two decades, it is still a very important country; a disaster here is not a fire across the sea but one that could affect just about everyone everywhere.

The original version of Takashima's book was divided into eight chapters. I have added this "Translator's Foreword" and an "Epilogue for the English Edition," written by Takashima and myself, which discusses some developments since March 11. As such, the English version of this book is organized into the following ten chapters. Following the foreword is the introduction, which was in the original edition; it begins with Takashima's experiences during the 1995 Great Hanshin-Awaji Earthquake, which occurred in his hometown of Kobe, and it explains how he used these insights when writing his later best-selling books, including *M8* (Magnitude 8), *TSUNAMI*, and this one in 2004, 2005, and 2006 respectively.[17]

Chapter 1, "A Megaquake in Tokyo," first looks at the respective estimates of the Japanese central government and Tokyo Metropolitan Government (Tōkyōto) with regard to a large-scale destructive earthquake hitting Tokyo or its surrounding areas. Takashima, who is critical of the unrealistically low figures presented (as am I), particularly as they relate to the numbers of dead and injured, then discusses ten different issues and factors not considered in the government reports. He warns that more realistic estimates, which consider a wide range of comprehensive and complex situations, are necessary, as are more preparations in light of new insights.

Chapter 2, "The Problems That Will Emerge Following the Megaquake," examines a variety of issues, from the handling of bodies and debris to criminal activity, fraud, rumors, and irresponsible and unhelpful media chasing stories; bothering victims amid their grief, despair, and exhaustion; and failing to help keep the public informed through accurate, objective, and timely information. He also challenges the myth that Japan is as safe and advanced as some would believe it to be.

Chapter 3, "Trench-Type Megaquakes," discusses the history of earthquakes in Japan and points out the seriousness that trench-type earthquakes present for the country. In particular, the chapter focuses on the Tokai earthquake scenario and includes a discussion about the stability of Japan's nuclear facilities, including the Hamaoka Nuclear Power Plant (Hamaoka Genshiryoku Hatsudensho), which sits above a major fault.

Chapter 4, "Tsunami," discusses the dangers that tidal waves present and looks at the history of Japan's experiences with tsunamis. It looks at estimates of tsunami heights nationwide, the challenges with coastal evacuation, the problems of underground malls and subways, and the failure of Japanese government authorities to fully come to terms with the increasing vulnerability of modern coastal cities.

Chapter 5, "Disaster Prevention and Disaster Reduction," introduces the Tachikawa Disaster Base (Tachikawa Kōiki Bōsai Kichi) and state of preparations by the central government and Tokyo Metropolitan Government before discussing the role of the Self-Defense Forces and the historic problems in the legislation and lack of political leadership in adequately utilizing them. In this chapter

Takashima also discusses the need to protect information, buildings, and industry, as well as the need for all citizens to take appropriate measures to educate themselves and prepare their homes and surroundings.

Chapter 6, "What the Government of Japan Is Doing Now and Should Continue to Do in the Future," examines the various organizations and committees involved in earthquake prediction and preparedness, arguing that they need to be realigned into a much more efficient and effective system. Takashima introduces the efforts of other countries in the areas of prediction, preparedness, mitigation, and response. He suggests that Japan needs to especially invest in disaster readiness and mitigation and strengthen its response capabilities, as earthquake prediction is at best a reactive approach to disasters.

In the conclusion Takashima briefly reintroduces some of his main arguments and concludes with a reminder to the reader that each person must become more knowledgeable about disasters and how to prepare or respond to them as we may not be able to rely on the government entirely for a variety of reasons.

The epilogue provides an update on events following the March 11 disaster, especially some of the major studies with regard to disaster predictions and planning that have emerged since. Several important books have come out about the March 11 disaster in the previous two years, and the reader is encouraged to review them. This chapter focuses more on the Japanese government's becoming more realistic and more open-minded to a variety of potential scenarios. Such changes are critically important so that it can never say again, "The scale of the disaster was unexpected [sōteigai]," like many officials did after March 11.

Hindsight is 20/20, and neither Takashima nor I wish this book to be an "I told you so" type of work, but instead we hope it will be a call for even greater efforts at preparing, sharing, and coordination in the years, months, weeks, or days before the next major disaster.

On an editorial note, as the reader would have already noticed, Japanese names appearing in this book are written with family name first, followed by personal name, as is Japanese custom. The original Japanese name of unusual or important organizations and titles is provided when it first appears. The notes at the end of the book were added by the translator as annotations to provide additional information, including some (but by no means extensive or full) comparisons with the March 11 disaster.

In conclusion, I wish to thank the following: Takashima Tetsuo for agreeing to let me translate this book and working with me in seeing it to completion; Kondō Takashi, his assistant, for helping track down answers to questions that came up and making the arrangements for the various meetings and interactions Takashima and I had throughout the project; Daniel Ihu, a student at the University of Hawaii at Manoa and freelance translator; Satō Fumiya, a student at Waseda University (Waseda Daigaku) who participated in an internship I created in my office at the Marine Corps Bases Japan, now Marine Corps Installations Pacific, for assisting with the initial translation of some of the chapters; my wife Emiko and children, Ami and Kennan, for their unconditional love and support especially during and after Operation Tomodachi; Lieutenant General Glueck, Maj. Gen. Peter J. Talleri, Maj. Gen. William D. Beydler, Maj. Gen. Mark A. Brilakis, Brig. Gen. Craig C. Crenshaw, Brig. Gen. Craig Q. Timberlake, Col. Leo Falcam, Col. Joel R. Powers, Col. Christopher P. Coke, and Col. Grant Newsham for the confidence these outstanding Marine Corps leaders placed in me. I also especially wish to thank my then direct supervisor, Col. Jonathan T. Elliott, Assistant Chief of Staff, G-7 (Government and External Affairs), Marine Corps Base Smedley D. Butler, and my current supervisor, Col. William J. Truax, and Col. Jonathan D. Covington, Assistant Chief of Staff, G-3/5 (Current Operations), now deputy commander, of the same staff, as well as Col. John C. Wright, then Chief of Staff, who have strongly supported my efforts to expand relations between the Marine Corps and vulnerable communities throughout Japan in the area of disaster cooperation.[18] I wish to thank everyone involved in these efforts as well, particularly my colleagues on the Butler staff, including Lt. Col. Katō Takenori, who assisted tremendously during Operation Tomodachi as the then GSDF liaison officer to III MEF, and Lt. Col. Yamamoto Masami, the current liaison officer, who has helped with our continuing relationship with Oshima Island in Kesennuma City, as well as in our disaster cooperation outreach with communities in other parts of Japan.

In addition, special thanks go to my former academic adviser, Dr. Iokibe Makoto, who has been actively involved in making recommendations on Japan's disaster preparedness and response capabilities, having himself experienced the Kobe earthquake, and more recently in serving as the chairman of the Reconstruction Design Council (Fukkō Kōsō Kaigi), established to advise Prime Minister Kan and prepare recommendations for him following the March 11 disaster for the long-term rebuilding of the Tohoku region. Within hours after the earthquake, we were in contact and sharing information and ideas. We stayed in touch afterward, obviously, and I had the chance in February 2012 to give a talk entitled "Operation Tomodachi and After" at the Hyōgo Earthquake Memorial 21st Century Research Institute (Hyōgo Shinsai Kinen 21 Seiki Kenkyū Kikō) in Kobe, for which Dr. Iokibe also serves as vice president and research director. Similarly my deep gratitude goes to former Cabinet vice minister Azuma Shōzō and Yonetsu Hitoshi, former member of Parliament and special adviser to Mr. Azuma, for their friendship and outstanding support behind the scenes in facilitating the work of the U.S. forces in Operation Tomodachi, particularly at Sendai and Yamagata Airports. My deep respect goes to Mr. Sugawara Hironobu, serving Oshima Island District in the Kesennuma City Assembly, for his work during and after the earthquake as a key liaison with the Marine Corps. Since then he has continued to work closely with us, helping us to understand the lessons learned and the status of the recovery efforts. He has also been a key supporter of our homestay program, by which the marines and sailors and their families of III Marine Expeditionary Force/Marine Corps Installations Pacific (at the time Marine Corps Bases Japan) brought children from Oshima Island to Okinawa for several days of rest, relaxation, and cultural exchange.[19] Moreover, I would like to thank Dr. Kawakatsu Heita, governor of Shizuoka Prefecture, for initiating the dialogue with us and for his cooperation to date, including inviting me to speak before his staff on a similar topic. Likewise I would like to thank Gen. Oriki Ryōichi,

Chief of Staff, Joint Staff; Gen. Hibako Yoshifumi; and Gen. Kimizuka Eiji, former and current Chiefs of Staff, Ground Self-Defense Force respectively, for the opportunity to work together over the years and especially in Operation Tomodachi. Likewise I appreciate the efforts of Col. Hiroe Jirō and his staff in the Japan-U.S. Coordination Cell at Camp Sendai, as well as those of Col. Yamaguchi Kazunori, then commanding officer of the Central Readiness Regiment (Chūō Sokuō Rentai) in Utsunomiya City, for his support in the early stages of the U.S. response and for the bravery demonstrated by his unit's work in Fukushima, and I wish them the best of luck in the future as they continue to capture the lessons learned and build on the bilateral relationship that was deepened there.

I would like to dedicate the English version of this book to two friends lost in the 1995 Great Hanshin-Awaji Earthquake, Kudō Jun and Mori Wataru, who were classmates at Kobe University, and to all the victims of the Kobe and recent Tohoku disasters, especially those from Oshima Island. May your deaths not be in vain. I promise to work toward ensuring they are not.[20]

Introduction

Each of us has a moment in life that cannot be forgotten. In the evening before my moment, I was in the Sannomiya district of Kobe, the capital city of Hyogo Prefecture (Hyōgoken). Some friends had arranged a party to congratulate me for an award I had won at the end of the previous year from a magazine recognizing a novel I had recently published. Living to the west of Kobe, I had gotten home late and was still asleep when I heard a loud noise, and I immediately jumped up. Still dark, the entire room was shaking. I was now sitting straight up in bed, but I could not manage to stand.

No sooner had the room stopped shaking when it started again. The bookshelf began rumbling, and books went flying off the shelves. When the trembling stopped at last, I attempted to get off the bed to stand. The floor was covered with books and other things, and I had difficulty opening the door. I was finally able to get it partway open and hurried to check on my children.

Outside it was still dark. There were no lights, no electricity. We huddled around the kerosene stove, in the dark, waiting for dawn. However, the sun never came out. The city beyond the mountains to the east was ablaze, and the sky above us was cloudy with that smoke.

January 17, 5:46 a.m. Kobe completely changed at this point. It was the beginning of the Southern Hyogo Prefecture Earthquake (Hyōgoken Nanbu Jishin), otherwise known as the Great Hanshin-Awaji Earthquake (Hanshin-Awaji Daishinsai).

I used the following wording to describe the scenes in Kobe in *M8*, a novel I published in the summer of 2004 about a magnitude 8 earthquake that directly strikes Tokyo:

Kobe is said to be in bad shape, and I turned on the television, but they are not showing Kobe, or at least not the Kobe I know. The elevated expressway has tipped over. A bus is dangling from the collapsed portion of the road. The local roads are covered on both sides with debris piled high, like mountains of collapsed homes and buildings. Black smoke is rising from the city. People are walking around in whatever they were wearing—usually pajamas—at the time the earthquake hit, covered in dirt and mud, walking sort of aimlessly. I wondered for a moment which country had now bombed us and realized it was in fact post-earthquake Kobe. It was completely destroyed. . . . I also worked hard to clear debris. It was the first time I had witnessed such destruction up close and seen dead bodies and of course touched one. After a while, I became used to handling the dirt-covered bodies of people I did not know. I had lost all sensation. I had never been amid such tragedy and had not experienced the fine line between life and death like this before.[1]

In fact this quote, and the one that follows next, reflect what I myself saw, heard, and felt during the Kobe earthquake: "A woman, in pajamas with disheveled hair, was just standing there dazed. A child was sitting in the street, crying. A man was digging through debris with his bare hands. An old woman was looking at the mud-covered body of a loved one, probably her husband, who had been found under the collapsed roof of their home."[2]

The concerns about an earthquake of magnitude 7 or above on the Richter Scale directly hitting Tokyo, as well as the ocean trench earthquake scenarios off the Pacific coast of Japan—known as the Tokai earthquake scenario, Tonankai earthquake scenario, and Nankai earthquake scenario (depending on where the earthquake originates)—have taken on an air of reality.

After I released M8 in August 2004, an earthquake occurred in September off the Kii Peninsula near Wakayama Prefecture in the Kansai area of the country, and in October a major earthquake hit the Chuetsu area in the middle of Niigata Prefecture, on the Sea of Japan side of the country. These were followed by a December 2004 earthquake in Sumatra, Indonesia, and a March 2005 earthquake to the west of Fukuoka Prefecture, in Kyushu, the westernmost of the main islands of Japan.[3] In particular, the magnitude 9.2 Sumatra earthquake was very deadly, causing unprecedented destruction.[4] The megaquake generated a tsunami that took more than 220,000 lives. At least 40 of my fellow countrymen were confirmed to have died there. In addition, there was a large earthquake in northern Pakistan in October 2005, registering magnitude 7.6 and killing more than 70,000 in that country and neighboring India.

In my novel *TSUNAMI*, which was published in December 2005, I explored the situation of a similarly large tsunami hitting Japan:

I saw the tsunami at the same time I heard people screaming they saw it. The top of the wave went right over the breakwater. The huge devil of a tsunami then went on to the roadways, swallowing up cars. People who had jumped out of their vehicles and run across the road disappeared in an instant. Others tried to climb up embankments and hillsides. When the tidal wave receded, there were no signs of anyone. . . . More than half the buildings that were on the coast were lost, and those that remained standing sustained substantial damage. Many places inland, along the coastline, are also still under water. It is hard to believe these places are in Japan. The beautiful sand of the coastline has been replaced with mountains and mountains of debris. Homes that were initially carried out to sea by the tsunami have washed up on the shore. Amid this debris are probably a lot of [bodies].[5]

Sadly it is entirely possible that Japan will experience scenes like this one and the one described below, also from the same book, in the not-too-distant future.[6]

It is said that there is no "if" in history. This is almost certainly true in our lives as well. Nevertheless, we are still likely to question things that have happened and will always do so, especially when we lose a loved one, friend, or neighbor to a tragedy such as an earthquake or tsunami. We ask ourselves, "What if she had not slept next to that large shelf?" "What if he had fixed his house to make it earthquake-proof?" "What if they had slept on the second floor rather than on the first?" "What if he had fled to higher ground?" They would still be alive, with their families, we imagine, saddened and angry by the loss.

Natural disasters and human disasters are different sides of the same coin. It is important not to forget about the earthquakes of 1995 and 2004 [and now 2011]. The valuable lessons learned from them need to be acted on. This is the one thing, almost like a memorial, we can do for the victims of the disasters.

In *M8* I suggested the following scene in Tokyo after "the big one": "Tokyo Tower and other skyscrapers, expressways, everything changed with the earthquake. The atmosphere changed at that moment."[7]

And in *TSUNAMI*, I wrote the following:

The people on the coast turned their backs to the rising wave and started running as fast as they could. They finally understood what was happening. Screaming, crying, and shouting for help, they ran. There were a lot of people gathered near the steps of the breakwater. So many that others could not get close to the steps. A huge wall of white was coming from the horizon. It was clearly visible. The wall of water consumed dozens of boats along the shore and started tearing up the beaches, approaching farther inland. An outdoor stage area, with people grabbing onto the steel stage structure, was picked up and carried off. Screams got louder. The roof of the outdoor stage suddenly appeared to stop and then sank under the water with the people still clinging to it. . . . A small fishing boat was lifted up on the wave and was heading into the port. The rudder would not work. A small tanker was overturned with its hull exposed. It had been lifted up onto the docks during the first wave of the tsunami. The fishing vessel was about to crash into the tanker. There were about ten people near the front of the tanker. When the two small ships collided, not only did the metal-on-metal cause a terrific sound, but also the collision ignited the fuel and an explosion occurred much like fireworks going off.[8]

MEGAQUAKE

CHAPTER 1

A Megaquake in Tokyo

Reports of the Tokyo Metropolitan Government
and the Central Disaster Management Council

According to Japan's Earthquake Research Committee (ERC; Jishin Chōsa Iinkai), there is a 70 percent chance of a magnitude 7 earthquake occurring within thirty years in the southern Kanto area known as the Earthquake Directly beneath Tokyo (Tōkyō Chokkagata Jishin).[1] Some consider this probability to be high and some consider it low. Ways to view things vary a great deal. However, we had better pay attention to this prediction.

In 1997 the Tokyo Metropolitan Government's Disaster Prevention Council (Tōkyōto Bōsai Kaigi) completed research and released its findings as the "Report on Predictions of Earthquake Damage in the Earthquake Directly beneath Tokyo."[2] In drafting the report, the committee considered different simulations using the following conditions:

1. The estimated epicenter is beneath one of four areas: the central part of Tokyo, the Tama district (to the west), the border between Tokyo and Kanagawa Prefectures (to the south), or the border between Tokyo and Saitama prefectures (to the north).
2. The earthquake has a magnitude of 7.2 on the Richter Scale.
3. The epicenter is about twenty to thirty kilometers below the surface.
4. The bedrock destroyed covers an area of forty kilometers by twenty kilometers.

5. The earthquake happened on a winter day, in clear weather, with wind velocity of six meters per second, at 6:00 p.m.

In the case of an earthquake directly below the metropolitan area that causes the most damage to Tokyo, there will be an earthquake registering 6-weak to 6-strong (on the Japanese seismic scale) that causes damage to 73 percent of the Tokyo metropolitan area.[3] The number of dead, according to the report, would be 4,732 killed in fires, 1,753 in collapsed buildings, 13 in train derailments, 189 crushed by debris, and 30 in landslides, for a total of 6,717. Similarly the report states the number of injured would be 111,900 in the quake, 23,907 in fires, 797 in derailments, and 221 in landslides, for a total of 136,825.

In August 2004 I published a book titled *M8*, which was about an earthquake directly beneath the Tokyo metropolitan area. When I was writing it, I often used materials citing the aforementioned predictions. However, I began wondering if those figures were really accurate. I cited them anyway. But now I regret having done so.

The number of deaths from the Great Hanshin-Awaji Earthquake was 6,433. More than 80 percent of these deaths were caused by victims being crushed under collapsed buildings or houses and fallen furniture. Ten percent burned to death. The rest were due to falling roof tiles and the collapse of nearby houses, walls, and other heavy items along the roadway, such as vending machines. More than 10,000 people were seriously injured, and 33,000 were slightly injured. So at least 40,000 people were hurt in total.

The main reason for these numbers of casualties has to do with the time that the Great Hanshin-Awaji Earthquake occurred. The Southern Hyogo Prefecture Earthquake (the academic name for that earthquake) occurred at 5:46 a.m., when most people were asleep. There were few people or cars on the streets.

What would it have been like if the Great Hanshin-Awaji Earthquake had occurred in the daytime? Expressways, railways, and underground shopping malls would have been seriously damaged, and the number of casualties would have been many times greater. It is entirely probably that the number of those crushed to death would have exceeded the number given above. The circumstances of the earthquake would have been completely different.

On September 1, 1923, an earthquake of M7.9 (intensity 6 in the Japanese seismic system) occurred in the Kanto area of Tokyo and neighboring Kanagawa Prefecture. The epicenter was Sagami Bay. The number of dead and missing reached 105,385, with 109,713 houses completely collapsed and 212,353 destroyed by the fires that broke out. This disaster was known as the Great Kanto Earthquake. In it 34,000 of 40,000 people who evacuated to an open area called Honjohifukushoato were burned to death.[4]

Common sense dictates that the extent of damage would be much more serious than the predictions indicated by the Tokyo Metropolitan Government if an earthquake as powerful as the Southern Hyogo Prefecture Earthquake occurred in Tokyo today. Indeed the simulation used by the Tokyo Metropolitan Government set the time of the earthquake at 6:00 p.m. If that were the case, where in the world did the simulators come up with the number of only thirteen dead from train, subway, monorail, and Shinkansen (bullet train) derailments in the middle of rush hour, when people have started to return home from work or trips or are going out to dinner, parties, and dates? On what did they base this estimate?

Eight million people live in the twenty-three wards of central Tokyo. The population density there is 13,000 people per square kilometer. There are more than 3 million households, 2.8 million cars registered, more than 7 million people using the Japan Railways (JR) in the city every day. In contrast, in the smaller cities of Kobe, Ashiya, and Nishinomiya—the most devastated areas of the Great Hanshin-Awaji Earthquake—there is a total population of approximately 1.4 million. The population density is 5,400 people per square kilometer. There are 528,000 households and 525,000 cars registered and more than 430,000 people using JR per day in the Hanshin area. (These figures obviously do not even include those using the other train lines or other train stations in the area.) The numbers for Tokyo are 5.7 times larger in terms of population than those in the Hanshin region, five times larger in terms of car numbers, and seventeen times larger in terms of JR users. The number of

JR Sannomiya Station users per day in the heart of Kobe—the most crowded station in the Hanshin area—is 120,000. In contrast, more than 750,000 people per day use JR Shinjuku Station (in western Tokyo). And there are many large-scale subway systems, underground shopping malls, and buildings in general.

Considering the fact that the Great Hanshin-Awaji Earthquake occurred early in the morning—a time that caused comparatively minor damage—the extent of destruction would be much more serious than the predictions made by the Tokyo Metropolitan Government if an earthquake as powerful as the Great Hanshin-Awaji Earthquake were to occur in Tokyo at 6:00 p.m.

It is true that it is difficult to accurately predict the extent of earthquake damage. A large city is composed of both old and new buildings, complex transportation networks, and different regional cultures. Men and women of all ages live there, and predicting their movement is next to impossible. However, it is even a bigger problem to announce such figures when the predictions are not necessarily sound. The report prepared by the Tokyo Metropolitan Government faced these challenges and used figures from neighboring prefectures, as well as all sorts of opinions and discussions.

In December 2004 the Earthquake Working Group of the Central Disaster Management Council's Experts Committee on Measures for an Earthquake beneath the Nation's Capital (Chūō Bōsai Kaigi Shuto Chokka Jishin Taisaku Senmon Chōsakai Waakingu Gurūpu), sponsored by the government of Japan, announced its prediction of the degree and location of damage in the case that an earthquake occurred directly in the twenty-three wards and neighboring areas of Tokyo. A couple of months later, in February 2005, the group followed this study up with predictions for the economic damage of such a disaster.

The working group looked at the following three earthquake patterns and conducted studies using eighteen different epicenters:

A magnitude 7.3 trench earthquake occurs where the North American Plate and the Philippine Sea Plate meet.

An earthquake of at least a magnitude 7 occurs along an active fault, such as the Tachikawa fault, in which the epicenter is close to the surface.

A magnitude 6.9 earthquake occurs below metropolitan Tokyo, or in nearby cities in Kanagawa, Saitama, or Chiba Prefectures, or under Tokyo International Airport (Haneda) or Narita International Airport.

Based on these situations, the working group announced its findings with regard to the degree of shaking or trembling that would be felt. According to the predictions, an earthquake of intensity 6 or higher on the Japanese seismic scale would hit a wide swath of the metropolitan area, and in some areas a quake of intensity 7 would hit.

Intensity 7 is the highest classification indicated by the Japan Meteorological Agency, or JMA (Kishōchō). (There are ten classifications, with 7 being the highest; see http://en.wikipedia.org/wiki/Japan _Meteorological_Agency_seismic_intensity_scale.) Intensity 7 was observed in the October 2004 Niigata-Chuetsu Earthquake (magnitude 6.8 on the Richter Scale) in some areas. Due to the degree of shaking, people are helpless to move when an intensity 7 earthquake occurs. Even buildings that are made of reinforced concrete and highly resistant to earthquakes may lean to one side or be severely damaged. The wall tiles and windows of most buildings are broken in earthquakes like this. There would be cracks in the ground and landslides. Indeed even the configuration of the ground may change.

There are three particularly worrisome types of earthquakes where damage is expected to be great. The first one is a North Tokyo Bay earthquake, in which an earthquake occurs between tectonic plates. This is an earthquake whose epicenter is in the boundary of the plates that lie in Tokyo and Chiba Prefectures. On the supposition that the earthquake is a magnitude 7.3 and its epicenter is twenty to thirty kilometers below the surface, the eastern half of Tokyo's twenty-three wards and Urayasu City (population 160,000) in Chiba Prefecture would be hit by a quake of intensity 6-strong, and the surrounding areas would be hit by a quake of intensity 6-weak.[5]

The second type is the West Tokyo metropolitan area earthquake.

This is an earthquake assumed to occur in Shinjuku (where the metropolitan government headquarters are) and the surrounding area.

The third type is the East Tokyo metropolitan area earthquake. This is an earthquake assumed to occur in Kasumigaseki (the heart of the central bureaucracy of the government of Japan, where the Ministry of Finance [Zaimushō], Ministry of Foreign Affairs [Gaimushō], Ministry of Internal Affairs and Communications [Sōmushō], and other important agencies are located) and the surrounding area.

In the latter two scenarios the assumption is that the earthquakes are each magnitude 6.9. According to the above-mentioned studies, the worst case would be a West Tokyo metropolitan area earthquake occurring at 6:00 p.m. with a wind velocity of fifteen meters per second. It is predicted that thirteen thousand people would die and two hundred thousand would be injured. However, this prediction is slightly optimistic since it estimates that the number of those dying in traffic-related or mass-transportation accidents would be only three thousand in the evening rush hour.

The bases for these damage estimates are the results of the Great Hanshin-Awaji Earthquake and the Great Kanto Earthquake. However, are we really able to get accurate damage estimates simply by studying these two earthquakes? As mentioned above, there is a big difference between Tokyo and Kobe in the scale of the cities, and there are big differences in almost every aspect of daily life between the Tokyo of today and that of eighty years ago. On top of this, the degree of damage in a large-scale disaster in a metropolitan area fundamentally varies according to the location and time that the disaster occurs.

Both the Tokyo Metropolitan Government and the central government anticipate, in their respective studies, that most of the casualties will be caused by fire and the collapse of buildings. This prediction is likely due to the fact that they both referenced the two big earthquakes of the past. Even if the previous examples saw such deaths, are such assumptions credible today or in different scenarios? In other words, each situation is different, and the estimates must better reflect the differences.

If the conclusion is right that the highest number of fatalities will be of those crushed to death, it means that regardless of whether someone lives in the city or in the countryside, the time from evening to the early morning hours, when people are sleeping at home or getting up to leave in the morning, will be the most vulnerable. However, if an earthquake hits a large city such as Tokyo, there will still be a large number of fatalities for reasons other than those discussed above.

According to the damage predictions of the Central Disaster Management Council, the following causes were considered regarding injuries and deaths: (1) collapse of buildings; (2) landslides along inclined slopes; (3) fires; (4) collapse of concrete walls and falling objects; (5) traffic/mass transportation accidents; and (6) damage at train stations and other mass transportation hubs.

However, there is a note in this report that those predictions did not take into consideration the following issues: deaths caused by a large-scale landslide, such as a mudflow; deaths caused by the difficulty for firefighters to reach an area or those evacuating from it due to traffic congestion, including abandoned vehicles and collapsed houses and buildings on the roadways; damage caused by falling electronic wires along railways and expressways; panic caused by the earthquake and outbreak of fires, causing crowds to rush into train stations.

There are other situations that could very well occur when normalcy is lost and people are unable to think calmly or clearly. The predictions of the Central Disaster Management Council, therefore, lack meaning since these unexpected situations or contingencies were not taken into consideration.

Regarding serious damage to traffic and transportation lines in the Great Hanshin-Awaji Earthquake, a 635-meter section of the Kobe route of the Hanshin Expressway (Hanshin Kōsoku Dōro) fell over. This occurred because eighteen reinforced concrete pillars and bridge piers collapsed. If the Great Hanshin-Awaji Earthquake had occurred two hours later, during the morning rush hour, there would have been many cars on this expressway and pedestrians, cars, motorcycles, and scooters underneath it in the area.

One scene—of a bus hanging off the Hanshin Expressway—made

international news and is a symbolic photo of the Kobe earthquake. In the photos and video images seen at the time, the bus seemed to dangle in the air over the collapsed section. What would the casualties have been like if an earthquake had occurred in the much more crowded Tokyo during the daytime? It would not be difficult at all to imagine that there would be a high number of casualties considering the amount of traffic and people nearby and potential for accidents. At this stage the accuracy of the calculation is not a big deal; it is the realization that there will be many casualties. Other numbers and figures are not so accurate either, and thus rough estimates will do. The short answer is that there will be a lot of deaths.

In places where people gather, such as movie theaters, concert halls, and stadiums, the collapse of buildings, as well as the ensuing panic, will take a heavy toll in human lives. The number of those who are crushed to death and injured in doorways, stairs, and escalators in buildings will certainly exceed the number of those involved in the falling of vending machines and concrete block walls.

In the Great Hanshin-Awaji Earthquake many collapsed buildings and fallen signboards blocked roads and walkways. A major earthquake in the daytime would find many people working in commercial buildings and the streets crowded with people and cars coming and going. Buildings filled with people would collapse, and debris would rain down on the people and cars on the streets. It is clear that there would be a large number of deaths and injuries. There would be many traffic accidents caused by cars whose drivers have lost control, and one can easily imagine them bursting into flames and causing fires. Similarly there would be trailers and tanker trucks on the roads carrying combustible materials and chemicals. I do not know if these scenarios are categorized as traffic accidents or extensions of building damage. However, they should be taken more seriously than comparatively small accidents such as the tipping over of vending machines and the collapse of the shoulder-high concrete block walls that surround many homes, schools, and buildings in Japan, as suggested in the report.

There were many fire-related casualties in the Great Kanto Earthquake. In contrast, most of the casualties in the Great Hanshin-Awaji

Earthquake were victims of collapsed houses. And there may be a new type of emergency or tragedy we haven't thought of in an earthquake in today's very modern and very large cities. It is not good enough to discuss prevention methods for collapsed houses and buildings, the outbreak of fires, or the tipping over of walls. We have to think out of the box and try every means available in order to reduce the potential damage.

In other words, if time and money are going to be spent doing such studies, they should be more realistic and helpful. The total amount of damage predicted for an earthquake directly beneath the Tokyo metropolitan area is 100 trillion yen ($1 trillion).[6] If that is the case, then investing in accurate disaster estimates and prevention is well worth it. Incidentally, according to the Ten-Year Reconstruction Committee (Fukkō Jūnen Iinkai), the expenses for rebuilding following the Great Hanshin-Awaji Earthquake reached 16 trillion yen (about $160 billion).[7]

In February 2005, as noted, the above-mentioned Earthquake Working Group of the Central Disaster Management Council announced its predictions for the economic fallout in the case of a powerful earthquake in Tokyo's twenty-three wards and surrounding areas. Assuming it occurred around 6:00 p.m. in winter with a wind velocity of fifteen meters per second, the direct economic losses would be 66 trillion yen ($660 billion) (55 trillion yen in building damage and 11 trillion yen in other damage of property and infrastructure), and indirect economic losses would be 45 trillion yen ($450 billion) (39 trillion yen in a decline in production and 6 trillion yen due to lost opportunities as a result of traffic and trade limitations). The worst case would be 112 trillion yen ($1.12 trillion) in losses in a year, which is 1.4 times as much as the national budget (fiscal year [FY] 2005) and 20 percent of Gross Domestic Product (GDP) (also FY 2005).

An earthquake that is as powerful as magnitude 7.0 to 8.0 can induce several times—maybe ten times—more damage than the preceding prediction since many elements, such as the urban design, population density, and social behavior of the residents, are intricately involved, depending on the area.

It is very difficult to say that the damage prediction reports for an earthquake in or immediately around Tokyo produced by the respective Disaster Prevention Councils of the Tokyo Metropolitan Government and the government of Japan are realistic. Furthermore, according to recent surveys, it has become clear that the thickness of the Philippine Sea Plate is ten to twenty-five kilometers thinner than traditionally thought. The tectonic plate, which was thought to be fifty kilometers in thickness in the mountainous areas around Kanto, is actually twenty-four kilometers in thickness, and the plate off the coast of Urayasu in Tokyo Bay, which was thought to be thirty kilometers in thickness, is in fact only about twenty kilometers. Both the Central Disaster Management Council and the Tokyo Metropolitan Government assume in their disaster studies that an earthquake would occur along the boundary of the Philippine Sea Plate. Since it has become clear that the Philippine Sea Plate is overall closer to the surface of the earth, the actual situation is far more serious than the earlier predictions.[8]

In the following sections I would like to examine some of the unique elements that the aforementioned reports did not consider in the big cities.

What Will Happen to the Railways and the Shinkansen

On October 23, 2004, a Shinkansen named Toki No. 325, which had left Tokyo that afternoon and was bound for Niigata City, derailed in Nagaoka City, Niigata Prefecture, at 5:56 p.m. This accident was the first case ever of a bullet train derailing since the establishment of services in 1964. (The train was traveling on the Joetsu Line, connecting Tokyo and Niigata itself; the line opened in 1991.) The bullet train was traveling at a speed of 200 kilometers an hour when a major earthquake occurred. The train continued 1.6 kilometers after its derailment and eventually stopped. Twenty-two of forty wheel axles were out of joint, and windows were cracked and broken. However, fortunately, the 154 passengers on board were uninjured. The line was reopened on December 28 the same year.

This derailment of the bullet train symbolically tells us how powerful the Niigata-Chuetsu Earthquake was. It also brought to an end the myth that the Shinkansen, until then without derailments or serious accidents, was completely safe. A massive earthquake in Tokyo will likely cause great damage to the railways and Shinkansen lines.[9]

In the Great Hanshin-Awaji Earthquake a total of sixteen trains in service in the Hanshin area derailed. Fifty passengers and six train operators were injured. Fortunately no one died in these accidents. The reason so many trains escaped harm and so few passengers were injured had to do with the fact that the earthquake happened so early in the morning (5:46 a.m.) and there were not many trains running at the time.

Of the fourteen trains operating in the area hit by the intensity 7 quake, thirteen trains, or 93 percent of them, derailed. Some experts in natural disaster damage prevention argue that approximately 1,100 passengers would have been killed and 10,000 passengers would have been injured in the region if the Great Hanshin-Awaji Earthquake had happened at around eight in the morning during commute hours. However, this figure does not include passengers on the Shinkansen line, which also travels through the Hanshin area.

There are 300 commuter trains in operation and 2,060,000 passengers on board during rush hour every morning in the twenty-three wards of Tokyo, running every one to two minutes on lines where there are shorter time intervals. The distance between trains is so short that it is almost impossible to stop in time to avoid collisions, no matter how quickly the conductor responds to apply the brakes. Considering the derailment percentage of the Great Hanshin-Awaji Earthquake, a large number of trains will likely derail in a similar situation in Tokyo, causing many crashes. Elevated railways are especially dangerous. There are 696 kilometers of rail lines in Tokyo. Twelve percent of them, or 84 kilometers, are on elevated structures.

Damage would be acceptable if the accidents were limited to derailments and all trains actively stopped operating, but what could happen—especially in urban Tokyo, with the very tight train schedules and many trains moving at the same time—is that a train that had been spared derailment might plow into the back of one that had derailed or otherwise crashed. If a train filled with passengers derailed, there would be many injuries, but if that train were hit by another train, also filled with passengers, the tragedy would be many times worse. Moreover, if part of an elevated structure were to collapse and a train fell below, pedestrians and people in cars underneath would also be involved and badly injured. If trains derailed and crashed into residential areas or other buildings, it would be that much more of a disaster too.[10]

The Tokyo Metropolitan Government predicts, in the survey mentioned above, that thirteen people would die and approximately eight hundred people would be injured in railway facilities in a megaquake. However, these figures are not at all realistic.

The Shinkansen train line handles earthquake damage prevention measures in two ways: one is to maintain rail tracks, and the other is to bring trains to a stop soon after an earthquake has been sensed. Of the 550 kilometers of the Tokaido Shinkansen line between Tokyo and Shin-Osaka Station (Osaka Prefecture), 297 kilometers or (54 percent) are built on embankments, 127 kilometers (23 percent) are on elevated structures, 71 kilometers (13 percent) are tunnels, and 55 kilometers (10 percent) are bridges. Some 296 kilometers of this line are being fortified to withstand a Tokai earthquake scenario. The bullet train Nozomi, incidentally, races along this line at a maximum speed of 270 kilometers per hour.

In the Great Hanshin-Awaji Earthquake some parts of elevated bridges collapsed and rail tracks floated in midair, suspended between sections. Eight bridges collapsed completely. Although the bullet train reduced its speed as a result of the earthquake and eventually stopped, there might have been a disaster if it had traversed the damaged portions.

With these lessons learned, steel plates six millimeters thick around bridges were added to help earthquake-proof them. However, by 2004 only 12,700 bridges had been reinforced, at a cost of 20 billion yen ($200 million). Five thousand bridges still needed to be reinforced, and the construction was to be completed by 2008.[11] One additional problem that needs to be considered as well is the liquefaction of the areas where bridges stand.

Bullet trains are equipped with the Yuredasu system, an emergency stop function that makes a real-time decision to minimize the effect of a natural disaster. Fourteen seismometers are positioned along the Shinkansen line. These pick up the first vibrations of an earthquake, called a "P-wave." The Yuredasu then stops electric transmission and automatically puts the brakes before a follow-on "S-wave" hits the Shinkansen line. All of this is done within the space of two to three seconds.

In the Niigata-Chuetsu Earthquake, the Yuredasu automatically applied the brakes at the same time that the conductor put on the brakes by hand. However, the train still derailed and traveled for almost another two kilometers before finally stopping on the bridge. The railway tracks on that stretch had been turned inward and outward and were split at multiple sites due to the earthquake. As mentioned above, twenty-two of forty wheel axes had come off while the bullet train was still moving, and eight of the ten cars derailed. The Yuredasu functioned as it should have, but the performance was not good enough, as the epicenter was essentially directly beneath the path of the bullet train, and thus the P-wave and S-wave reached the sensors at about the same time.

The bridge reinforcement construction that had been done following the Great Hanshin-Awaji Earthquake contributed to the fact that there were no injuries in this derailment accident. Some observers point out that the train did not tip over because it was traveling in a straight line and the cars were the older, heavier versions. It is also fortunate that there were no trains coming from the opposite direction. However, what do you think would happen to the bullet train Nozomi, which is forty tons—approximately two-thirds of the sixty-ton Toki—and which passes through lots of curves and operates at short intervals with many trains coming from behind and in the opposite direction?

In the case of the Joetsu Line Shinkansen derailment (the Toki train), there was a possibility of that train colliding with one heading for Tokyo since the trains pass one another closely and Toki No. 325 traveled quite a long distance after it derailed. One shudders to think what would happen if two bullet trains crashed into each other without having been able to reduce their respective speeds.

It takes one minute and a half and a braking distance of four kilometers for the Nozomi bullet train to completely stop after the emergency brake has been applied if it is traveling at maximum speed. If there is a place where elevated railroads or bridges have collapsed, trains could fall into the rivers or valleys below.

Kiyono Junji, a professor of earthquake and lifeline engineering at Kyoto University, created a simulation in which an earthquake occurs directly below a Shinkansen line as a Nozomi train, carrying 1,300 passengers, is passing above. Although the train applies the emergency brakes, some of the train, still traveling at a speed of 150 kilometers per hour, falls through a gap in the tracks where a bridge has collapsed. According to Kiyono's simulation, the first four cars of the Nozomi would fall from the elevated bridge, and the rest of the cars would derail and crash into one another. It is almost the same as a car accident when the passengers are not wearing their seat belts. Most of the passengers on the Nozomi would be fatally injured. It would be even worse if a train were coming up from behind or from the opposite direction and they touched or otherwise crashed into one another.

The most terrifying Shinkansen scenario is an accident in a tunnel or on a bridge. It is very frightening to think about a situation in which a bullet train derails and stops in a tunnel and is then scraped by or collides with a train coming from behind or ahead.

It was long believed that mountain tunnels, as they were dug through solid bedrock, were safe in an earthquake. However, in the Niigata-Chuetsu Earthquake, rail lines were raised by ten centimeters in a hundred-meter stretch of the track, and some concrete pieces fell from the ceiling in the Uonuma Tunnel collapse. There were reports that a one-square-meter part of the tunnel had fallen and landed on the tracks. This all occurred on a relatively new train line, so we must inspect some of the older lines as well.

"It was a coincidence that no one was injured," an official with the Ministry of Land, Infrastructure, and Transport (MLIT; Kokudo Kōtsushō) said, commenting on a report by an investigative committee looking into the derailment accident of Toki No. 325. A crowded bullet train, traveling at a speed of a hundred kilometers an hour, crashed head-on into the debris—rocks, dirt, sagging electric wires, and collapsed utility poles—that had piled up on the tracks ahead as a result of the earthquake. The report noted that the rail lines, which were not supposed to break, were in fact ruptured. The report concluded that the rupture of the rail joints was due to multiple impacts of the earthquake and derailment. Moreover, the committee concluded that the fact that there were "no injuries was simply the result of a series of coincidences" and pointed out the danger of a collision had a train been coming in the opposite direction.

JR Tokai (otherwise known as JR Central) brought in a new system called the Tokaido Shinkansen Line Earthquake Early-Warning System (Tōkaidō Shinkansen Sōki Jishin Keiho Shisutemu) in August 2005, or Terasu. The fundamentals of this system are almost the same as those of the Yuredasu system described above. The main difference is that Terasu is an improved version of Yuredasu and thus is able to reduce the time between the detection of an initial P-wave and the issuance of a warning by one second. Simultaneously JR Tokai increased the detection points of Terasu earthquake recorders along the Shinkansen line and extended the area of automatic speed control by earthquake recorders in order to increase the ability to reduce the damage caused by earthquakes.

Subways Are Even More Dangerous

The collapse of the myth about the safety of the Shinkansen was one of the topics of discussion at the time of the Niigata-Chuetsu Earthquake. However, there has been no loss of life in Japanese subways ever since their opening in 1927, and they also boast a high record of safety. This is in large part as a result of the adoption of the Automatic Train Stop (ATS) system and cars made of noninflammable material.

Although it was a severe earthquake registering intensity 7, the damage in subways during the Great Hanshin-Awaji Earthquake was limited to a few people being injured. However, this was because the earthquake occurred before six o'clock in the morning. Just six trains were running and only one derailed. However, there were accidents where subway cars scraped against the outer walls of tunnels due to their collapse and the shaking of trains. Doors and window frames were heavily damaged due to these kinds of accidents.

It is said that the shaking underground in an earthquake is less severe than above ground. However, the platform pillars were crushed and the ceiling collapsed in Daikai Station, an underground station of the Kobe Rapid Transit Railway (Kōbe Kōsoku Tetsudō). A train had passed through this station just before it collapsed.

In the Great Hanshin-Awaji Earthquake there was much damage in places where the road-laying method (*kaisaku koho*) was used to build the subways. With this method subways or their stations are built by digging down from the road surface. The total length of subway tracks in Tokyo is 239 kilometers, and 70 percent of them were built by this road-laying method.

The earthquake damage in a subway system would be like that from an earthquake occurring in a train and an underground shopping mall at the same time. Even if the trains safely made emergency stops, passengers would be left in the tunnels. They would have to make their way out of the trains and to the underground stations, from which they would have to get outside. They would have to do this all without panicking or rushing, causing injury to themselves and others.

The tunnels have an emergency power supply in them, but no one knows if this power supply will actually work properly in the case of an earthquake. Passengers would be in the dark if the cables got unhinged or the emergency power supply was somehow disabled. If aftershocks occurred or something fell on the passengers or had already fallen from the ceiling, they could be injured or disoriented. Moreover, if another train was traveling through the tunnel at the same time, a tragedy would occur if people were hit by the it. Many would be killed.

Underground subway passages in Tokyo are very long, and underground stations are often multileveled. Fortunately there are not many combustibles in the passages, but the station precinct could be filled with smoke and people could become hypoxic once a fire broke out. In addition, poisonous gases might leak out. Without a functioning ventilation system, a lot of people could die. On top of these possibilities is probably the most dangerous situation of all: flooding in the underground subways, enclosed as they are.

The Tokyo Metropolitan Government–run subway, the Toei Asakusa Line, and some other lines are old, and some reinforcement construction is being done at many places along these lines. What is very scary, however, is that the line runs under the Sumidagawa River, along the river and coastal area of Tokyo Bay. If the surface above the subway lines were to crack due to an earthquake, the subway tunnels would crumble. Even a small crack would cause water to rush in at a rapid rate, and the tunnels, lines, trains, and stations would be destroyed fairly quickly. What's more, most of these stations are connected to underground shopping malls.

In addition, the Tozai, Hanzomon, Yurakucho, Shinjuku, and Oedo Lines all either go under or along the various rivers in Tokyo or along Tokyo Bay. One leak will result in the submersion of all or most of Tokyo's subways.

Officials are making water holding tanks to help alleviate the flooding that would occur, but the source of the water flooding into the subways would be Tokyo Bay and, behind it, the Pacific Ocean. These tanks may help a little, but it would be only a matter of time before the subways and parts of the city became flooded.

It must be remembered that rescue operations for victims in subways are, under ordinary circumstances, many times more difficult than operations on the surface. Such operations would be further complicated if some or especially if all of the aforementioned problems arose. We have all used the subways at some point. Just thinking about what it would be like to be trapped below, in the tunnels and in the dark, during an earthquake makes one shudder.

Expressways Become "Tunnels of Death"

The Metropolitan Expressway Company (Shuto Kōsoku Dōro Kabushiki Kaisha) has the following manual on its website.[12]

> What are we supposed to do when we are driving on the Tokyo Metropolitan Expressway and are suddenly hit by an earthquake? Follow the guidelines below:
>
> (1) Slow down slightly, park your car on the left, and turn off the engine.

(2) Collect information about the earthquake and the traffic using the radio.

(3) Do not drive the car from that time on.

(4) Follow the directions given by the police and the public corporation officials.

However, suppose we are hit by an earthquake of intensity 6 when we are driving at a speed of about a hundred kilometer per hour. Unlike what is suggested in the aforementioned manual, we would not in fact be able to control our car at that point. Cars would not be able to stop no matter how firmly the driver put on the brakes since the cars would probably be bouncing around or even be airborne. Moreover, yours would not be the only car on the road; there would be other cars, perhaps many cars, around you. Some would be traveling in the same direction at very tight intervals. Once a car hits a wall or brushes against another car, there will be a pileup with a lot of cars involved. Tractor-trailers filled with goods might barrel over cars in front of them and tip over, spilling out their goods over the expressway. A tanker filled with gasoline might then crash into this pile and ignite it. People would be walking and running around. Others, trapped in their flaming cars or vans, would be struggling to get their seatbelts off. Some vehicles might explode. Scenes such as these would be repeated throughout the region.

One of the symbols of the Great Hanshin-Awaji Earthquake was the 635 meters of collapsed expressway along Route 2. Eighteen of the support pillars broke and caused the expressway to fall over. This road was built in the 1960s. There is a possibility that similar types of highways in Tokyo might collapse if an intensity 7 earthquake were to strike.

In Kobe after the earthquake we saw many pillars whose external walls had broken, exposing the reinforced iron rods inside. The external walls had cracked due to the initial shock of the earthquake, and as these cracks got bigger, the iron rods pushed out. Made fragile from the quake, the rods were no longer able to support the weight of the expressway, and they collapsed.

Also in the Great Hanshin-Awaji Earthquake, part of the expressway collapsed. The photo of the bus dangling over the edge best captured this disaster. Miraculously the bus driver and passengers were able to escape certain death.

The Tokyo Metropolitan Expressway, otherwise known as the Shuto Expressway, opened in 1962 with a 4.5 kilometer stretch of road, and it has extended out radially since then. No matter how much the original section, now nearly fifty years old, is reinforced, it is still vulnerable.

Accidents can also happen in the tunnels. In July 1979 seven cars were involved in a pileup of multiple collisions in the Nihonzaka Tunnel on the Tokyo-Nagoya Expressway in Yaizu City, Shizuoka Prefecture. A fire broke out, and seven people died and three were injured. It was a tragedy, but it could have been worse.

In the above-mentioned case the first collision occurred at a point that was 420 meters from the exit of the tunnel. Some cars braked and stopped, but other cars continued to come into the tunnel one after and another and became trapped, not able to move at all. In the end 173 cars and buses, which were 60 meters from the original crash site, burned. The fire ignited leaking gasoline and freight that was in trucks, such as polyethylene and pine resin. Temperatures in the tunnel reached 800–1,000 degrees Celsius. Vehicles that were far away also were burned.

Even the best emergency equipment at the time was useless. The fire burned for sixty-five hours. It took one week to reopen one lane and sixty days for operations at the tunnel to return to normal. The economic loss from this accident is said to have been 6 billion yen ($60 million).

There are twenty-five tunnels within the Tokyo Metropolitan Expressway network. The longest is the Tamagawa Tunnel, Bayshore Line, which runs 2,170 meters. The second is the Kawasaki Koro Tunnel, which is 1,954 meters long. The third is the Chiyoda Tunnel, which is 1,900 meters long and extends over the Inner Circular Route (C1) and Fourth Shinjuku Line. And there are some other tunnels that are more than 1,000 meters long, such as the Yaesu, Kuko-kita, and Tokyo Port (Tokyokō) Tunnels. These tunnels may become "tunnels of death" when accidents or disasters occur.

Underground Shopping Malls Are Not Safe

There are underground shopping malls of fourteen thousand square meters in Kobe City, such as Sanchika (below Sannomiya Station) and Duo Kobe (below Kobe Station). They were hit by an intensity 7 quake in the Great Hanshin-Awaji Earthquake. Surprisingly there was no serious damage, such as collapsed walls and pillars, but there were of course display cases that tipped over, broken windows, cracked tiles, goods and products thrown about inside the stores, and bent shutters in front of the shops.

Because of the relatively light damage sustained by these two underground shopping malls, it is said that underground facilities are more resistant to earthquakes. However, we may not be able to say that if an earthquake occurred not in the early morning but in the middle of the day, when the malls are filled with customers. A lot of mothers would be with their small children, and elderly people would be running their errands.

Although underground shopping malls are equipped with emergency power sources, temporary blackouts are inevitable. When an earthquake occurs, darkness sets in. Display cases would tip over, the displayed goods would hit people, and ceiling tiles and lights or glass would probably rain down on people in the stores or walkways. There is a possibility that a fire or two might break out. Just at the moment the lights came back on, people would be rushing to the doorways. It is obvious that panic might ensue. Hundreds, perhaps thousands, of people would rush to the doorways amid the broken glass and other debris in the passageways. Not all doors would open. Someone might fall in the stampede. Many people might be crushed to death.[13] What would complicate the situation further would be if the auxiliary power failed to go on due to cables snapping in the earthquake or something else damaging the equipment. Chaos would ensue, and it would be hell on earth.

There are thirteen underground shopping malls in Tokyo, and their total floor space is 2.26 million square meters. That space is sixteen times as large as Kobe's, and the layouts are more complicated.

Worse yet, a lot of people would run into underground facilities to flee from broken window glass and signboards that would rain down on them in the outdoor areas such as those at Shinjuku and Shibuya. This flow of people would crash into those already in the underground malls, perhaps at the entranceways and exits.

Fires in underground shopping malls are especially frightening. Although these underground malls are equipped with sprinkler systems, it is likely there would be a lot of smoke and perhaps poisonous gases caused by the fires. No one can tell what will happen in a large-scale earthquake in a large metropolitan city.

Oil Storage Tanks and Gas Stations on Fire

A lot of people probably remember the photos of the oil storage tanks on fire in Tomakomai (Hokkaido Prefecture in the northern part of Japan) with their thick clouds of black smoke. The fire was caused by an earthquake that occurred off the coast of Tokachi in September 2003. A long-form periodic quake hit the area of Tomakomai, about 260 kilometers from the epicenter, and a fire broke out. Naphtha in the tanks was shaken by the long-form periodic quake, and the iron covers slid to one side. Naphtha leaked from the tanks, and a spark caused by the friction between the covers and the containers ignited the naphtha and set off an explosion. The tanks burned for the next forty-four hours.

In the case of the June 1964 Niigata Earthquake, which was felt in Tokyo as well, fires broke out in four oil-refining and storage facilities, and tanks ended up burning for twelve days. In the case of the earthquake off the coast of Miyagi Prefecture in June 1978, an oil storage tank caught fire. The cause of all these fires was something known as the sloshing phenomenon, in which a leak of naphtha developed because of the slow long-form periodic quake.

The probability of liquefaction and land subsidence by an earthquake in the Tokyo Bay area is high. The problem not only has to do with the quake resistance of a storage tank, but it also involves countless pipes. There may be some problems in a disaster, especially with the pipe joints. Pipe joints are said to be able to bear the strain if they are less than one meter apart. However, joints may be completely destroyed if multiple disasters happen simultaneously, such as land subsidence and liquefaction.

There are thirty-three large-sized gas tanks and thirty-four large-sized oil storage tanks in Tokyo. Moreover, throughout the capital city's twenty-three wards there are many storage tanks of flammable liquids, such as gasoline and naphtha, and tanks of high-pressure gas. And there are many facilities and factories that deal in dangerous substances designated in the Fire Service Law (Shōbōhō).

The safety of a system as a whole is much more important than that of individual equipment in an industrial complex. Since petrochemical complexes import oil from overseas, most of those facilities are located along the shoreline. The ground along the shoreline is soft and prone to liquefaction. It is likely that a tsunami would hit these areas as well.

In 1976 the Industrial Complex Disaster Damage Prevention Law (Sekiyu Konbinaato Tō Saigai Shōbōhō) went into effect. It prescribes that industrial complexes have to be equipped with water-cannon trucks, chemical fire engines, and foam firefighting carriers. However, massive fires with which those special fire engines cannot deal have already broken out to date. Accordingly some companies have brought in mass storage foam cannons made in the United States. These cannons can put out large fires in a short amount of time, releasing 30,000 liters of water per minute at a distance of 150 meters. This type of equipment demonstrated its capability in the June 2001 fire at a 100,000-ton gas tank at Orion Oil; the fire was put out in just sixty-five minutes.

According to the investigation on the petrochemical complex fire in the Tokachi coast earthquake, 45 of 105 storage tanks were damaged by the quake, and 30 of them were seriously damaged or had developed leaks.

There are 13,209 outdoor tanks around the country, each with a capacity of 500 kiloliters (kl) or more. It is said that at the time of this writing more than 60 percent of them have not had earthquake resistance testing or were found to have had some problems in their ability to withstand earthquakes since they were not reinforced. If a Tokai, Tonankai, or Nankai earthquake scenario were to occur, fires could break out in any of those storage tanks. Moreover, firefighting would be much more difficult if a tsunami hit those coastal areas.

Fortunately there was no large-scale storage-tank fire or explosion in the Great Hanshin-Awaji Earthquake. However, there was damage to a fraction of the tanks, pipes, and fire-extinguishing equipment. There was a gas leak at the liquefied petroleum gas (LPG) facility in Higashi Nada Ward in Kobe, and twenty-eight thousand households and seventy-two thousand people were urged to evacuate in the neighboring areas.

There are more than six hundred chemical, petroleum, and coal factories in Tokyo, Kawasaki, and Yokohama.

Countless Numbers Killed by Fire

The number of victims who burned to death in Honjohifukushoato Park alone in the firestorms following the Great Kanto Earthquake is thirty-four thousand. Firestorms are created by the convection of heat and crosswinds under certain circumstances, and they move around, indiscriminately destroying buildings and houses while taking people's lives along the way.

According to the previously cited report by the Tokyo Metropolitan Government, fires will likely break out in all twenty-three wards at the same time after an earthquake occurs. The report predicts that more than 324,000 homes and other buildings would burn down. Although large-sized underground water tanks have been constructed in the wake of the Great Hanshin-Awaji Earthquake to facilitate firefighting, roads would be clogged with collapsed buildings, debris, and disabled vehicles, so fire trucks would likely have difficulty getting to the scene in the first place. In the Great Kanto Earthquake the flames rapidly spread to neighboring areas, and multiple smaller fires amassed to become one big firestorm, wiping out much of the area.[14] As soon as the shaking in an earthquake stops, it is important to check all possible sources of leaks and fires and extinguish flames or fires immediately.

In a densely built-up area, where residences, offices, stores, apartment buildings, and factories are mixed together, the roads to evacuation shelters would be blocked by fires or debris or both. In the Great Hanshin-Awaji Earthquake most of the roads that were narrower than eight meters were blocked. Moreover, many elderly people live in old residential areas in Tokyo. There would be countless numbers of victims in the fires as help would be unable to reach these and many other people.

In the Great Hanshin-Awaji Earthquake the lack of water hindered firefighting. This lack was due to the fact that underground water pipes broke in the earthquake and fire hydrants did not function properly. Learning these lessons, Kobe City has set up 246 earthquake-proof water tanks in public parks and pumps that can draw water from rivers. Also it has introduced ten-ton pumpers and fire engines that can convey seawater through their lines and system.

There were fifteen fires in the Niigata-Chuetsu Earthquake and 294 fires in the Great Hanshin-Awaji Earthquake. A large number of people in particular died from the fires in the Kobe earthquake. According to firefighters and other emergency responders, the comparatively small number of fires in Niigata was due thanks in part to the emergency drills that had been conducted and the fact that there were fewer gas leaks. In the Great Hanshin-Awaji Earthquake, on the other hand, underground iron gas pipes broke, and a spark ignited the leaked gases. In the case of the Northridge Earthquake in Los Angeles in January 1994 (magnitude 6.7) as well, broken gas pipes were the major source of the fires. Some experts point out that as a lesson learned following the Great Hanshin-Awaji Earthquake, iron gas pipes were replaced by those made of polyethylene, and as a result there were a small number of fires in the Niigata-Chuetsu Earthquake.

In the Kobe earthquake gas service to 860,000 homes came to a halt. There was a great deal of damage in low-pressure pipes that convey gas to residential households. Iron pipes broke, but those made of polyethylene did not. The polyethylene pipes are very flexible, and they would not break even if there was a one-meter change in the topography.

In the case of a fire in a multi-tenant building in the Kabukicho area, a red-light district in Shinjuku, Tokyo, in September 2001, forty-four people died in one building that had violated numerous fire codes. The fire burned for five hours. If an earthquake occurred, it would be highly likely that multiple fires would start in such crowded buildings, and the death toll would likely be far worse.

In February 2005 a fire occurred in Kita-ku, Tokyo, where construction workers were digging for a hot spring. The fire continued to burn for more than twenty-four hours. Fortunately no one was hurt. However, methane was discovered in the atmosphere nearby that was 460 times as dense as it ordinarily is. Methane gas had been blown up with water from 1,500 meters underground.

The estuary of the Arakawa River was once called the Tokyo gas field (*Tōkyō gasu den*). Gas had been exploited in that area until 1972. In other words, there are combustible gases in the ground in Tokyo. What would happen if an earthquake caused cracks in the ground and fire ignited gases blown out from those cracks?

Liquefaction and Ground Surface

Many people probably remember photographs of the muddy water over the roads and manholes that protruded tens of centimeters above ground. These photos captured the liquefaction phenomenon seen on Port Island in Kobe City following the Great Hanshin-Awaji Earthquake. It was after the 1964 Niigata Earthquake that the word "liquefaction" was used for the first time to explain this phenomenon. Many apartment buildings in Kawagishi Town, Niigata City, had tilted or collapsed due to liquefaction.

The ground is composed of various kinds of soil. Among the various particles in the soil are water and air. If an earthquake occurs, particles of soil are shaken and they become destabilized. The space among these particles, water, and air shrinks, and water moves to the surface. This is the phenomenon of liquefaction.

Liquefaction is likely to occur in wet areas near coastlines and rivers, reclaimed land that has not compressed well, and areas whose groundwater level is high. Liquefaction can cause the collapse of buildings. Water and dirt that come up onto road surfaces can not only obstruct emergency vehicle traffic, but can also weaken the roads themselves and push water pipes and gas lines to the surface.

It is well known that liquefaction is likely to occur in sandy areas that contain moisture. And there are many such areas in large cities.

Many of those areas are industrial zones and are equipped with storage tanks of oil and chemicals. There was a great deal of damage in port installations in Kobe.

Because of this situation, the Tokyo Metropolitan Government's Urban Planning Bureau (Toshi Keikakukyoku) has prepared guidelines about civilian construction as part of the metropolitan government's Disaster Prevention Policies Project (Tōkyōto Shinsai Taisaku Jigyō Keikaku), and they are found on the metropolitan government's website: "In areas where there is a danger of liquefaction, reinforcement of the foundations of wooden buildings by iron rods and multistory buildings by the driving in of stakes into firm, solid ground and some other methods, if necessary, are recommended. In the future we intend to strengthen anti-liquefaction measures by furthering construction confirmation inspections."[15] In addition, the Tokyo Metropolitan Government, on its website, also mentions that it is "adopting methods of reinforcing the buildings themselves, as well as strengthening the foundations under and around the buildings, when it constructs public buildings in the areas where there is a possibility of liquefaction."[16] The home page of the Yokohama City Office (Yokohama Shiyakusho) explains such measures in more detail in recommendations entitled "Our Home's Anti-Liquefaction Measures."[17]

Avoid Building in Areas Where Liquefaction Is Likely to Occur

Liquefaction is likely to occur in certain areas. When it is unavoidable to construct a building in such areas, mitigation measures can be put into place to help reduce the possible damage. Areas where liquefaction will likely occur: sandy ground whose underground water level is high; areas that previously were rivers, paddy fields, swamps, or the seashore.

Mitigation Measures

Reinforce the foundation. The most effective measure against liquefaction is to reinforce the ground or foundation underneath a building or road. From a study of past earthquake damage, it is noted that liquefaction damage would be reduced if the stratum two meters from the surface were strong and solid. Therefore, the most effective measure to prevent liquefaction is to reinforce the ground at this depth or replace the sand with something that is stronger against liquefaction.

Construct a strong building. Making a building of a simple shape helps to make it stronger in resisting earthquakes. Reinforcing the foundations of buildings is also an effective method against liquefaction.

It goes without saying that a building that is resistant to liquefaction is also one that would be resistant to earthquakes.

The number of deaths in the Great Hanshin-Awaji Earthquake was 6,433. As mentioned above, about 90 percent of the deaths were due to the collapse of houses and buildings, and about 80 percent of those were crushed or suffocated to death. These casualties were in what is called the "earthquake disaster belt," concentrated in the area between Rokko Mountain and the seashore. There are two theories to explain the label of "earthquake disaster belt." One is that there is a reverse active fault beneath the area. The other is that there was a "focusing phenomenon" in the area by which the shaking caused by the earthquake was concentrated between the softer and harder levels in the topography.

According to Takahashi Manabu, a professor in the Department of Geography, College of Letters, at Ritsumeikan University in Kyoto, "Many of the houses and buildings were destroyed in a line along a river. This line, in fact, looked like a snake. These houses and buildings meandered like a snake along a river."[18]

In short, we have to study the magnitude of an earthquake in terms of not only its distance to an active fault but also the influence of the topography.

The Niigata-Chuetsu Earthquake received much attention in the media because of the first derailment accident since the opening of the Shinkansen. However, one has to wonder if the Shinkansen was really safe all the time prior to the earthquake.

In the Niigata-Chuetsu Earthquake one bullet train derailed. No elevated bridges collapsed, fortunately. However, in the Great Hanshin-Awaji Earthquake eight bridges and elevated sections of the

Shinkansen's Sanyo Line (which runs between Shin-Osaka Station and Hakata Station in Kyushu) were considerably damaged. What would have happened if Shinkansen trains were running over those sections at that time? It might have been a disaster involving a few hundred people or a few thousand if it were later in the day. There were no accidents or fatalities with the Shinkansen then simply because luck intervened. The Great Hanshin-Awaji Earthquake was at 5:46 in the morning. A disaster was avoided because it occurred before the first Shinkansen departure of the day in that area.

It should be noted that the eight sections that collapsed were all at the intersections of old river channels and old river channels that had since been reclaimed. In other words, the ground in those areas was comparatively soft, and the earthquake happened to be more powerful or was felt more in those spots than in other places. In addition, as if to underscore this point, in areas along old river channels and on reclaimed land above old river channels, the degree of the damage to houses and buildings was more serious and there were far more casualties.

Many people tend to think that the earthquake damage was the result simply of there being an active fault. However, the influence of the ground is one of the elements that we cannot ignore. The following lists some famous earthquakes in Japan, with varying degrees of damage.

Genroku Earthquake in 1703 (M7.9–8.2)

An earthquake that hit the southern part of the Kanto region. Odawara Castle and the neighboring town were completely destroyed. Twenty thousand homes are said to have collapsed, and more than five thousand people died.

Ansei-Edo Earthquake in 1855 (M7.0–7.3)

Caused considerable damage to the Edo (historical name of Tokyo) area. It is said that more than seven thousand people died and about fourteen thousand houses collapsed or burned down.

Meiji-Tokyo Earthquake in 1894 (M7)

The damage was mainly in the area near Tokyo Bay. Some

twenty-four people died and twenty-two houses collapsed or burned down.

Great Kanto Earthquake in 1923 (M7.9)

A very powerful earthquake that hit the southern part of the Kanto area. The number of dead or missing was more than 105,385 (with some figures as high as 140,000), and at least 109,713 buildings were destroyed.

Those earthquakes are the ones that have hit Tokyo. Let's look at the terrain in the Tokyo area next.

To make it simple the terrain in the Tokyo area can be divided into four categories. The first is a plateau that spreads over the mountainous area of Oku-Tama. The second is a hill in the Tama area. The third is a plateau that spreads out from Tachikawa to Shinjuku. The fourth is alluvial lowland areas such as Chuō-ku, Kōtō-ku, Sumida-ku, Shinagawa-ku, and Ōta-ku. The hill was created by sediment from the Arakawa, Edogawa, and Tamagawa Rivers when the Ice Age ended about ten thousand years ago. Naturally older ground is more solid and can more easily resist quakes. On the other hand, the ground of plateaus and low-level lands is soft, and the shaking in an earthquake tends to be felt more. In the case of Great Kanto Earthquake many houses collapsed in the alluvial lowlands.

In addition, the amplitude of an earthquake increases when the quake reaches soft ground from solid ground. This means that a quake becomes stronger. The "focusing phenomenon" occurs around the boundary of the soft ground and the solid ground, causing a complicated reaction of reflections bouncing off and through each type of ground.

There are four tectonic plates around Japan—the Eurasian Plate, North American Plate, Pacific Plate, and Philippine Sea Plate. Tokyo, which will likely experience a major earthquake in the future, is located in the Kanto Plain area. The Kanto Plain lies on the North American Plate. The Philippine Sea Plate lies under the North American Plate. The Pacific Plate goes beneath those two plates from the east. The edge of the Philippine Sea Plate strikes against the Pacific Plate. On top of these three levels of complexity sits Japan.

There are said to be five different types of earthquakes that might occur in a scenario in which Tokyo is directly hit. The first is an earthquake that occurs near the surface of the North American Plate. The second is one that occurs on the boundary of the North American Plate and the Philippine Sea Plate. The third would be caused by the sinking of the inner part of the Philippine Sea Plate. The fourth is one that occurs on the boundary of the Philippine Sea Plate and the Pacific Plate. The fifth would be caused by the collapse of the Pacific Plate.

However, at the May 2005 Japan Geoscience Union meeting (Nihon Chikyū Wakusei Kagaku Rengō Gōdō Taikai), held in Makuhari, Chiba Prefecture, Toda Shinji, a researcher at the National Institute of Advanced Industrial Science and Technology (Sangyō Gijutsu Sōgō Kenkyūsho) presented a paper titled "A New Type of Plate Structure under the Kanto Area." In it the author noted that there was a new fragment or block after the Pacific Plate:

> The Philippine Sea Plate, which has been said to be deeply sinking under the Kanto Plain, actually only extends to the north edge of Tokyo Bay. In fact, another plate (that I call here a block) exists between the Philippine Sea Plate and the Pacific Plate. The block is 100 kilometers by 100 kilometers in size and is twenty-five kilometers in thickness. It is at a depth of 30–100 kilometers. It is located parallel to the Pacific Plate. This block appears to be the residuals of the Pacific Plate, which was fractured and was unable to sink any lower. (It is very interesting to note that the shape of the block and the Kanto Plain are the same.)[19]

It is interesting indeed. This square block covers all areas of Tokyo and the six neighboring prefectures of Chiba, Kanagawa, Ibaraki, Tochigi, Saitama, and Gunma. Toda explains:

> This fractured plate is very important when thinking about the likely occurrence of an earthquake whose epicenter is directly below the metropolitan area. Earthquakes whose epicenters are in the area between Ibaraki Prefecture and western Chiba usually occur at the surface, east edge, or bottom of this block. (This is

one of the so-called "earthquake nests.") There is a possibility that a powerful earthquake will hit the metropolitan area, like the Ansei-Edo Earthquake (M7.0–7.3) of 1855, which occurred where this block and the Philippine Sea Plate or Pacific Plate met (contact surface) and caused much damage.[20]

While the details are still being studied, it appears there certainly must be some correlation. Toda continues:

Earthquakes between the boundaries usually occur in water areas. However, in the Kanto area they occur directly below the surface of the ground. And since there is one extra plate between two plates, there are more areas of contact surface, and thus earthquakes occur more often in the Tohoku area and west of Izu. Also they will occur much deeper. There is a possibility that some earthquakes that were thought to have occurred in plate may be reviewed and reinterpreted as having occurred at the boundaries of plates. (However, it is clear that the East Chiba Prefecture Earthquake [Chibaken Tōhōoki Jishin], an M6.8 that occurred in [December] 1987[21] occurred within the Philippine Sea Plate.)[22]

Although Toda states that examining the matter further may be difficult, he points out that with his new theory, it has become much easier for scientists to explain what has taken place now than in the past, as the explanations then used to be unnecessarily complex and not convincing.

It is thought that it was near the Japan Trench that this block, a fragment of the Pacific Plate, emerged.

Plates usually move ten centimeters per year. Therefore, since it is about three hundred kilometers to the edge of this block found in Gunma Prefecture, it is speculated that this block emerged approximately 3 million years ago.

What has become clear is that the structure of the plates in the Tokyo area is getting even more complex, and no one can tell what will happen in the future.

Panic

The scene is a large sports arena, such as a soccer or sports stadium. The sound of a gunshot is heard. People scream and rush toward the exits. Many are crying. One person falls, and the crowd runs over him or her. We sometimes see this scene in movies. But what if it actually happened?

Suppose that we are in a department store and suddenly feel an earthquake. The power may be cut off, but the lights will soon come back on since the department store is equipped with an emergency power source. In an intensity 6-weak earthquake, unbolted furniture will easily jostle about and fall. Display goods will fall from their shelves and scatter all over the place. Display case glass will break, and there will be glass on the floor.

Now comes the difficult part. Elevators will not work, and people will be trapped. People will rush to escalators but will have to go through all of the scattered goods, broken display cases, and other debris on the floor. The escalators will not be working either, but at least they can be used as stairs. However, a lot of people will be rushing to them. Hundreds of people will make a rush for the exits. Once someone stumbles over something on the floor, the people following will also fall. This kind of accident will happen repeatedly.

It would be preferable if the store employees tried to calm everyone down and guided them safely to the exits, but it is entirely possible that the employees themselves will also panic. Moreover, first-time customers will have difficulties understanding the layout of the store.

If an emergency were to happen at the Tokyo Dome, as many as fifty thousand people would make a rush to the exits. Some people might fall down on the stairs, and tens if not hundreds of people might crush them. Worse yet, the entrances and exits of the Tokyo Dome are revolving doors. Although there are doors for emergency use, confusion at the scene of the panic is inevitable. What would happen if the power supply were cut off during a night game? Moreover, people would further panic in such a situation if something were to fall down from the ceiling.

If we are at a baseball stadium or other outdoor sports complex, it is probably best to stay put until the earthquake stops or go out onto the field to be safe. However, the situation will be completely different if thousands of people start to panic. When thinking about the damage in an earthquake that occurs in the daytime, we must keep in mind that there will likely be many people who die, sadly, as a result of being crushed to death during a mass panic.

It is very important for us to make sure of where the emergency exits are when we are in movie theaters, concert halls, and event sites.

Foreigners in Tokyo

There were ten thousand Swedes and five thousand French visiting Sumatra for the sun and fun during their Christmas vacation in December 2004. There were many other foreign nationalities there too.

One of the features of the Sumatra earthquake was the high proportion of foreign dead. About 5,400 corpses were found in Thailand at the end of January 2005. About half of them were foreigners. Many tourists come to Sumatra Island from all over the world, including Japan. The Sumatra quake was in the middle of the Christmas holidays, and most of the foreigners were from European countries.

In most cases the victims who were killed in the tsunami did not have their IDs, such as passports. Indeed most were stripped of their clothes by the tsunami. Since the affected areas involved seaside resorts, some of the victims had been dressed lightly in only bathing suits or shorts. Under these circumstances identifying the dead was very difficult. Furthermore, many problems arose due to the differences in religion and customs with the way the bodies were handled.

What if this kind of big disaster happened in Tokyo? About 2 million foreigners reside in Japan.[23] An additional five hundred thousand are said to be illegal residents who did not go back to their own countries after their visas expired or who were smuggled into Japan, and they lack proper official identification. Most of them stay in the big cities, where they blend in somewhat better. It is believed that half of the illegal aliens live in Tokyo.

Most of the illegal aliens are Chinese, but they also come from a wide range of countries. They live in crowded area such as Shinjuku and Ikebukuro, which are said to be vulnerable to disasters, both natural and manmade, due to their narrow streets and mixture of buildings, some of which have been known to violate building and fire codes.

Illegal residents do not possess a foreigner's registration card (*gaikokujin tōroku shōmeisho*), or at least not a valid one, so it may be difficult to confirm who they are or where they live. In the Great Hanshin-Awaji Earthquake there were many deaths among students and those who were living alone. There were cases where neighbors did not notice missing neighbors, as they assumed they had evacuated. If foreigners died in natural disasters such as earthquakes, they could end up being categorized as "unidentified," particularly if they were illegal aliens.

Inquiries about safety will flood in from overseas. Japan may lose its credibility as a responsible, caring, modern nation if it cannot respond to such inquiries in a timely and compassionate manner. The Immigration Bureau (Nyūkoku Kanrikyoku) of the Ministry of Justice (Hōmushō) and the police must be prepared to deal with the problem of how to deal with foreign people living in Japan during a disaster, as well as with their relatives and embassies or consulates asking about them.

Needless to say, this situation applies to people who are Japanese citizens as well since Tokyo and other cities are inherently places where a large number of people gather who are not originally from that area or who may just happen to be visiting or just passing through when disaster strikes. So even though a victim may be Japanese, it might be hard to identify the body. Identifying bodies or remains in the September 11, 2001, terrorist attacks in the United States and the Sumatra earthquake and tsunami was very difficult. In the case of the 9/11 attacks, with most bodies completely dismembered, DNA examination was undertaken by private professional organizations. It cost approximately $10,000 per body. We should always carry our IDs with us as long as we are living in Japan. Even if we escape death, without some form of ID, life would be very hard in the days and weeks after a disaster. This is especially true for foreign residents legally living in Japan.

In the Great Kanto Earthquake there were rumors that Koreans were going to cause riots, and as a result, as many as six thousand Korean people and others mistaken for them were murdered by vigilantes. When people are in the depths of despair over having lost a family member or their home or belongings, a minor misunderstanding, a rumor, or some misinformation could cause them to lose their senses altogether, resulting in more tragedy. We must not repeat the same mistakes.

Unfortunately there are many criminal groups composed of foreigners in Japan. It is thus possible that crimes such as looting and robbery will increase in the chaos after a disaster. Of course, the same can be said regarding Japanese criminal gangs.

In the Great Hanshin-Awaji Earthquake the overseas media made it appear as if no crimes had occurred in the disaster area. However, there were in fact crimes such as burglaries in vacant homes and shops and other incidents.[24] Tokyo, as an international city, will have to work extra hard to maintain public order after a major disaster.

However, in the Great Hanshin-Awaji Earthquake foreign people in the disaster areas and Japanese residents alike helped each other and worked together for the reconstruction of their community. Moreover, many people shared the feeling that they had all suffered and were in it together, regardless of nationality or race.[25] Mankind came together in Kobe.[26]

CHAPTER 2

Problems That Will Emerge Following a Megaquake

Deaths Will Be in the Tens of Thousands

Ten days after the December 26, 2004, Sumatra earthquake, the *Sankei Shimbun*, which had sent reporters to the scene, observed the situation in the following way:

> As of January 5, there are 1,474 bodies here in Ban Muang Temple on the outskirts of Khao Lak, in Panga Province in southern Thailand. Approximately 1,000 have had DNA samples taken, and these are in a refrigerated container. The taking of DNA samples from the remaining 400 corpses has yet to be completed. The doctors are working especially hard to prevent the spread of infectious diseases. Thai authorities are worried about the outbreak of cholera due to the large number of flies that are attracted to the decomposing bodies, and they disinfect the corpses once a day. The medical workers handling the bodies wear two layers of gloves and masks, protective clothing, and long boots, and they do everything they can to protect themselves. When people leave the morgue area, they and their vehicles are disinfected.[1]

People walked through the wreckage with masks on, holding their noses. In a large open area of the town, those killed in the disaster were lined up in body bags. This is how things looked as a result of the earthquake and tsunami. In the disaster that took more than two hundred thousand lives, bodies are still trapped in the debris.

Bodies that were dug out remained exposed in the open, with no one to take care of them. There were also many unidentified bodies at hospitals, schools, and other public facilities.

Moreover, a great deal of polluted water had entered wells and homes. Large areas of water remained after the tidal wave receded.

There was a great fear that unsanitary conditions and other health risks would increase in the countries most affected by the tsunami — namely, Thailand, Indonesia, India, and Sri Lanka. Not only were there no morgues to handle the bodies, but also the evacuees did not have toilets or drinking water and had to live in primitive conditions.

The sanitary conditions of Indonesia and India were already bad to start out with as they are developing countries, but as a result of the tsunami, they would clearly only get worse. The international community would have to work hard to protect the victims from malaria and other infectious diseases.

In the southern and eastern parts of Sri Lanka, the path of destruction is clear as one travels from the coast, through the towns, and even into the farmlands and lakes beyond. In areas that are low in elevation, the water has yet to recede. Debris and other matter are in these now filthy lakes, causing the sanitary situation to become bad. The local Red Cross, afraid of the outbreak of cholera, salmonella, and dysentery from the food and water in the area, is calling on residents to not drink or eat potentially unsafe water and food.[2]

In Japan there is less concern about these sorts of infectious diseases following flooding after a typhoon or a large earthquake. Instead what is of concern is the massive amount of rubble and wreckage. If debris is left around, there will be bad smells and serious sanitation problems that could get in the way of recovery efforts.

According to the *Yomiuri Shimbun*, Japan's largest newspaper,

While there are more than 3,000 bodies, none of the bereaved families have been able to come and get them as of January 19, three days after the Southern Hyogo Prefecture Earthquake. More tragic reports keep coming in announcing new death figures.

Schools, temples, and gymnasiums throughout the disaster-struck area are serving as temporary morgues for the deceased residents. People are asking that funeral services be held quickly for them. However, there are few undertakers that can help right now in the area, and bereaved family members have just been staying with the bodies, keeping vigil, sad or speechless. Meanwhile, their frustration is growing as they see the number of bodies piling up and the slowness of the local government's response while they wait in the bitter cold of these temporary morgues for help with burying their loved ones in a proper manner.[3]

Although it is not well known, there was an issue with cremations at the time of the Great Hanshin-Awaji Earthquake. There were some two hundred bodies in a gymnasium and sports complex. There were not enough coffins to go around. Bodies were wrapped in blankets, and the bodies were placed on futons.

Autopsies still needed to be performed on the bodies. Eighty percent of the victims died from being pinned under rubble. In other words, they were crushed to death. According to one doctor, there was no sign of pain or suffering on the victims' faces. This was because the homes and other structures in which they lived collapsed so quickly. There were other victims, however, whose arms were extended as if to prevent the ceiling or something else from falling on them. Curiously even though it was very cold then and the temperatures were around zero, the bodies began to decompose quite quickly, as if it were summer.

There were many bodies as a result of the Great Hanshin-Awaji Earthquake. Five thousand, five hundred bodies had to be taken care of quickly, but it was beyond the capability of the crematoriums in Hyogo Prefecture to handle them in a short time. As a result, chaos ensued. Some families personally took deceased family members to other prefectures to handle their cremation, such as the case of one couple who brought their deceased parents, laid out in the back seat of their car, over to Nara Prefecture, two prefectures to the east.

The crematoriums in the disaster area were able to handle 300 bodies per day. If crematoriums in neighboring prefectures in the

Kinki region were included, the number amounted to approximately 430 bodies per day.

The Ministry of Health (Kōseishō) issued a request to the neighboring prefectures, including Osaka, Okayama, Tokushima, and Kyoto. These prefectures agreed, but the problem was with transporting the bodies. Eventually, the Self-Defense Forces assisted in transporting them. The Ground Self-Defense Force carried 431, and the Maritime Self-Defense Force transported 9. Helicopters were also used to transport the bodies. The SDF personnel involved in transporting the deceased showed great respect and care. For example, they wore white uniforms and white gloves and laid sheets and blankets down on the floors of the large trucks. The trucks were large because the SDF did not want to have the coffins stacked up on top of one another. As a result, only six coffins were placed per truck.

However, even then, there were cases when cremated remains, which had been placed in cardboard boxes, were mistaken for trash and thrown out into garbage trucks.

The following introduces a section of one prefecture's disaster response manual that discusses searching for victims and handling their remains:

1. Sanitary Considerations and Community Feelings

It is necessary to handle the bodies in a proper manner as both a sanitary problem and a consideration of the feelings of the community at large. As such, it is necessary to secure and properly establish places for the remains; ensure proper identification procedures and communication with the police, media, and family members; and correctly and quickly handle at every stage of the process the remains of those who cannot be identified.

2. Establishment of a Cooperative Framework with the Medical and Dental Associations within the Prefecture

It is very important for the Prefectural Police Headquarters to establish ahead of time a cooperative relationship with the various medical and dental associations and other related organizations within the prefecture as it will be necessary to undertake autopsies and identify many bodies in the event that there is a major disaster with the loss of a lot of lives.

3. Establishment of a Framework for Disposal of the Bodies

Each city, town, and village should plan for situations when there may be a large number of deaths or when the crematoriums in the immediate disaster area cannot be used and seek the cooperation of local companies to acquire a large amount of dry ice, coffins, and urns in order to preserve the bodies while also working with other local communities in order to establish a framework for properly disposing of the bodies. In this situation the Prefecture (Health and Welfare Division) can assist the local cities, towns, and villages by making requests to the private sector and other prefectures.

The following section discusses looking for remains, physically retrieving them, cremations and burials, and payment of grievance compensation. While these may be uncomfortable topics, they must be faced in the event of a large-scale disaster. For this reason, such a manual is necessary.

Moreover, according to the Disaster Assistance Law (Saigai Kyujōhō), the remains of victims must be cremated within ten days of a disaster in order to prevent infections or other diseases from the decay of bodies.

In the case that the Tokai, Tonankai, and Nankai earthquake scenarios occur at the same time, it is estimated that victims will number in the tens of thousands. It is not impossible that the tragedy will be as extensive as that of the Indian Ocean tsunami. The government may already have prepared them and has just not informed the public about it, but perhaps there are more than ten thousand body bags in some storage area somewhere.[4]

The aforementioned scenario is one in which at least the bodies are found and can be cremated or buried and funerals can be held for the victims. There are many situations where no remains are left. For example, the September 11, 2001, terrorist attacks in the United States caused many to go missing. Only 1,585 of the more than 3,000 victims were identified. The remains, even fragments, of the rest of the victims were never found. Of those identified, 1,205 had to be identified through DNA tests, as only partial remains were found.

According to the following report, Setsu City in Osaka Prefecture is preparing a DNA bank of its residents in the event of the need to identify victims in a large-scale disaster.

In a large-scale disaster in which tens of thousands of people die, it will be difficult to identify bodies, as was seen at the end of last year in the Indian Ocean tsunami. In light of this difficulty, Setsu City has announced its decision to establish a databank to preserve the DNA of its residents. The system will use oral samples, but the main feature of the new system will be that it will be able to preserve these samples at room temperature. As a result, it will be possible to preserve the DNA at the city offices or even privately in one's home. Setsu City plans to preserve the samples in an earthquake-resistant vault. One reason for using this new system is that while dental records are often used to identify victims in a fire or crime, it is more difficult to do so when bodies are mangled, as in a disaster. Another reason has to do with the fact that in some cases, even if the DNA is accessible, often there is no comparative sample with which to match it, and the person goes unidentified.[5]

While there are proponents of the protection of personal information, it is hard to argue about the need to protect personal information when considering the degree of destruction in a large-scale disaster.

A Large Amount of Debris

"There is more than seventy thousand buildings' worth of debris," the *Yomiuri Shimbun* reported in late January 1995, following the Kobe earthquake.[6] "Moreover," it continued,

the rubble of the collapsed pillars of the Meishin Expressway, the bridges of the Hanshin train lines, and many other materials need to be disposed of. The director of the Environmental Division of the Hyogo prefecture government, Nakao Seiji, said that the rough estimates of the Ministry of Transport (Unyushō) and the Ministry of Construction (Kensetsushō) are that the amount of the debris is more than twenty Kasumigaseki Buildings, or approximately 10 million cubic meters. . . . He admitted that the biggest problem is the removal of the debris from buildings and private homes without the permission of the individual owners. This is complicated by the fact that insurance and other compensation claims are involved, as well as future urban planning requirements, so the prefecture is discussing these matters with the central government. "There is a need," the director stated, "for there to be a special law. It is necessary for an even speedier recovery."[7]

One can easily recall the tragic sight of the collapsed buildings and homes, the tipped-over expressway, and the sections of missing elevated railways. Everyone understands that the first step in the relief, restoration, and recovery process is to remove the debris. In particular this will allow for relief goods to flow into the region.[8] The Kobe city government estimated that the removal of debris would amount to 400 billion yen ($4 billion).

One of the problems with debris removal is precisely the issue of cost and who will cover it. According to another report in the *Yomiuri Shimbun,*

> The government announced on January 28 that the cost for the demolition of private homes and apartment buildings and the removal of debris for those that sustained substantial damage [*hankai*; literally "half-destroyed"] would be borne by the government and not by the individual owners. Initially the local government will undertake the demolition and debris removal, and the central government will underwrite half the costs. In addition, it was decided that the Self-Defense Forces would be actively used to help demolish, remove, and transport the debris. In this way, as in the case of the Great Hanshin-Awaji Earthquake, the government has gotten involved in helping to demolish and take care of damaged and destroyed homes and buildings. The central government understands that the local authorities are unable fiscally to pay for all of this and has responded positively.

In addition, it has agreed to cover local bonds issued by the cities and towns, and when it comes time to repay them, the central government will provide a portion of the national tax revenue allocated to local governments to them. As a result, it appears the central government is effectively covering approximately 80 percent of the costs for debris removal.[9]

If the amount of debris to be removed is 10 million tons and if four-ton trucks are being used, then it will take 2.5 million loads to remove it all. Not only is finding a place to dispose of the rubble challenging, but so is actually being able to transport it all. Traffic in Kobe after the Great Hanshin-Awaji Earthquake was chaotic, with the expressways completely closed and restrictions placed on driving on national roads at numerous junctures. Stickers and other signs were used for emergency and other official vehicles, but many were copied and used without permission.

Criminal Activity

In a disaster everyone is vulnerable. But it is the old, young, and women who are particularly at risk. According to the *Sankei Shimbun*,

> In the Province of Aceh, Indonesia, the most seriously hit disaster area, brokers and other human traffickers are increasingly active in taking many orphaned children amid the confusion caused by the tsunami. According to Associated Press reports, rich clients from Malaysia and Singapore are coming to Indonesia for the purpose of human trafficking. A public affairs official from the United Nations Children's Education Fund, or UNICEF, has confirmed at least one case of an attempted purchase of a child. Moreover, there are many cases in Indonesia where simple cell phones are being used to handle adoption cases. The Indonesian government has temporarily banned children under the age of sixteen from leaving the country. It has also sent police officers to the evacuation shelters in an effort to stop human trafficking. Moreover, according to reports from the British Broadcasting Corporation, there are cases, such as those in Sri Lanka, where the tsunami relocated land mines, increasing the level of danger

there, and sexual abuse is occurring in the evacuation shelters in India, where parents have abandoned their children after receiving financial assistance, and in Indonesia, where children have died from pneumonia after drinking dirty water.[10]

In addition, UNICEF announced shortly after the disaster in South and Southeast Asia that members of the militant separatist group, the Liberation Tigers of Tamil Elam, otherwise known as the LTTE or Tamil Tigers, which operated in northern Sri Lanka and has since been defeated by the Sri Lankan military, had kidnapped at least forty children from one of the refugee camps in that country and forced them to become "children soldiers." While one might think something like this could not happen in Japan, we have to realize that there are weaker members of society, especially young girls and older people, who are vulnerable.

In the wake of the Great Hanshin-Awaji Earthquake the foreign media often reported on the "order and discipline of the Japanese people" in times of disaster, and reporters noted they were impressed that they did not observe or hear of riots or looting. But this is not necessarily an accurate portrait of events at the time. For example, the *Yomiuri Shimbun* reported the following:

A series of burglaries took place at about twenty stores, including a precious gems shop, in the Sannomiya and Motomachi districts of Central Ward, Kobe City, amid the chaos immediately after the Great Hanshin-Awaji Earthquake. The value of the stolen items amounted to 100 million yen [$1 million]. According to Osaka and Hyogo Prefectures' police authorities, the stolen items appeared to have been traded in for money in Osaka City. In addition, some thieves using a truck went around to empty homes in the disaster area and robbed them of a lot of items. As a result of these incidents, local residents are forming neighborhood watch units and patrols. There are many heartwarming stories of neighbors as well as strangers helping each other in the disaster, but there are also these horrible crimes that are taking place at the same time. The police authorities in both prefectures are strengthening their efforts to prevent crimes in the area.[11]

There was a case of a man who went around advertising cheap apartments and tried to trick people into giving him money as deposits. The particularly despicable thing about this was that he was a public servant working for Kyoto City who had applied for time off as a "volunteer."

In Amagasaki City and Takarazuka City [both in Hyogo Prefecture], where a lot of homes sustained damage in the Great Hanshin-Awaji Earthquake, a national newspaper reported the following a few weeks after the disaster:

Repairmen are going around targeting victims of the disaster by signing contracts with them to fix their homes, lying to them by saying that the Disaster Relief Law can be applied to the contract to receive a 50 percent reimbursement, or people who are pretending to be volunteers are going around actually forcing people to purchase sheets to cover up their damaged roofs or other property in what is known as "disaster business" [saigai shōhō]. There are yet other examples of vendors going around saying they were requested by the city to obtain signed repair contracts in different neighborhoods. The Consumer Protection Centers [Shōhi Seikatsu Sentaa] in each city are calling on residents to speak with them or the police before signing any contracts, as they still may be shaken or troubled after the earthquake. The Consumer Protection Center in Amagasaki, where more than 4,500 homes and buildings were seriously damaged or completely destroyed, received thirty-two calls by the end of January on disaster-related matters. In particular, home and roof repairs are the biggest concerns of the callers. In the Higashi Sakuragi-cho district of the same city, a contractor from Osaka visited someone's home on January 27 and said he would be able to repair his roof. He said the cost would be 5 million yen, but he then falsely told the owner that with the disaster relief law it would cost just 2.5 million yen. They went ahead and signed the contract. The owner called the Consumer Protection Center afterward, and the center was able to have the contract annulled. There were also three cases in Amagasaki where contractors told homeowners that they had been sent by the city's water and sewage bureau to make repairs and then charged exorbitant amounts for their work. In Takarazuka there were thirteen cases of homeowners falling prey to contractors taking advantage of them. One person, who needed all the tiles to the roof of his house replaced, was told that it would cost 13.5 million yen, but if the owner let the contractors advertise their work as a "model home," they would reduce the cost to just 7 million yen. The homeowner went ahead and signed the contract. In another case a person showed up saying he was a volunteer and put a sheet over someone's home to protect the roof; later he sent a bill for his services amounting to 30,000 yen.[12]

While the media did not introduce the subject, there were reports of things being stolen from collapsed or damaged homes where the residents, who had evacuated, were no longer there when the robbery occurred. Of course in homes that were destroyed, it would be very hard to tell in the first place what was missing. There were also numerous reports of rape, including one rumor that a female volunteer had been sexually assaulted by a victim of the disaster who had lost his mind.

Not all the stories have been confirmed, and indeed it is hard to know what is true, but such reports suggest that people must keep their wits about them or some human tragedies may occur, like those that were seen in the wake of the Great Kanto Earthquake, when Korean residents were accused of poisoning the drinking water and then killed vigilante-style.

Rumors and Misinformation

At the time of the Great Kanto Earthquake residents from Korea (which had been annexed by Japan in 1910) in the Tokyo and Yokohama areas were accused of "poisoning wells," and as a result of the rumors some six thousand Koreans are said to have been murdered by vigilantes and others caught up in the killing spree.

At the time of the Great Hanshin-Awaji Earthquake many foreign residents were killed, injured, or suffered damage in some way. However, the majority of them worked with the Japanese hand in hand to help each other, and as a result a strong relationship developed. In addition, it is also true that more than 197 billion yen ($1.97 billion) was collected in donations, and volunteers came from all across the country (and the world).

Hiroi Osamu, a professor of disaster studies and human behavior at the Interfaculty Initiative in Information Studies at Tokyo University [Tōkyō Daigaku Shakai Jōhō Kenkyūsho] who was staying at a hotel in central Osaka from January 16 to attend the Fourth Japan-U.S. Workshop on Urban Earthquake Reduction [Nichibei Toshi Bōsai Kaigi], scheduled to begin the next day—the same day, coincidentally, as the Great Hanshin-Awaji Earthquake—said he awoke right away when he felt the very strong jolts of the earthquake. Hiroi entered the heavily affected Amagasaki, a city a few miles to the west of Osaka, six hours later. One of the things he saw when he arrived was a religious group or cult that was standing along the roadside, paralyzed with fear and pale in complexion, calling out that there would be another large disaster. "It is said that rumors usually start a few days after a disaster," the expert on human behavior in disasters told this newspaper, but even he was surprised at how fast information moved around the disaster area. Hiroi explained that "perhaps it has to do with the scale of the shock of the residents." Furthermore, the television networks and radio stations even reported on the morning of the earthquake that Takarazuka City Hospital [Takarazuka Shimin Byōin] had collapsed. This was incorrect. The particularly bad thing about this misinformation is that the hospital had 271 patients in it when the earthquake hit, and over the next several hours many more people needing emergency care were brought there. The hospital staff had to deal with phone calls from family and friends asking about their family members, believing that the hospital had collapsed, in the middle of trying to take care of arriving patients and ambulances. Moreover, hearing the rumors, a unit from Middle Army [located just south in the neighboring city of Itami] even showed up at the hospital adding to the confusion.[13]

In addition to these incidents, other rumors circulated as well, such as, "Tonight there will be a large aftershock" and "There will be a direct-hit earthquake in Osaka on the twenty-fourth." In other words, normally people would be able to see these rumors for what they were, but when they are already greatly upset, agitated, or worried, they are unable to remain calm. Some misinformation or rumor can cause them to act irresponsibly.

The preceding newspaper story continued as follows:

At the time of the Mt. Unzen Fugendake eruptions in Nagasaki Prefecture in 1991, some rumors started to emerge about a week after residents had evacuated that a gang of thieves from neighboring prefectures had entered the evacuation area, and many residents rushed back to their homes, which were in a danger zone due to the lava flows and other hazards. So many people returned to their homes to get their valuables that traffic jams ensued. According to Professor Hiroi, "There is the mentality that the first person to do something wins. Are we able to predict a direct-hit earthquake on Tokyo and get a jump on nature? We see this need for speed or to be first, too, in the applications for temporary housing or for compensation. We will likely see more rumors and false information when it comes to financial matters and where and how people live. These sorts of rumors can be prevented when the government and the media constantly provide detailed, correct information to the people."[14]

Regardless of whether it is widely known that it is impossible to predict a direct-hit earthquake, there was a great deal of misinformation relating to vacancies at temporary housing and to financial compensation. According to the *Yomiuri Shimbun,*

At one of the evacuation shelters in Takarazuka City a rumor was going around that "applications would not be accepted after the eighth" for identification certificates for victims of the disaster [*hisai shōmei*] whose homes had been seriously damaged or completed destroyed, and as a result more than 1,000 people showed up on the morning of the seventh at the city offices to make sure their application was received. The city offices were unable to handle all the applicants then and made the cutoff at 1,000. They gave numbers to the remaining people and had them come back the next day. They announced, too, that "there in fact was no deadline and not to believe unsubstantiated rumors." Identification certificates are necessary to apply for loans at banks or with insurance companies, as well as for tax relief. Takarazuka City has been receiving applications since January 24 and has issued 18,000 certificates over the past two weeks. The rumors about the deadline started about two or three days ago and were heard among victims in the evacuation shelters and other places. Over the past few days 1,000 people have been showing up daily to apply, and some forty city workers were mobilized on the sixth to deal with the applications, working late into the night. They issued 1,700 certificates that day. The city attributes this particular rush to rumors that the surge of applications to have one's home demolished for those with seriously damaged or completely destroyed homes was extended to the seventh or that the deadline for being issued a certificate identifying one as a victim of the disaster was to stop on the sixth.[15]

There were other rumors and misinformation out there. For example, "If you go to such-and-such a place, you will find water." "There is juice in such-and-such vending machine." "There is a free hot bath service started in Osaka." "If you have a driver's license, you can apply for temporary housing." "If you go to the city offices, you can receive compensation." In fact all of these rumors were just misinformation. Such rumors caused the phones to not stop ringing at the city offices, and people began carrying buckets to just go around in circles looking for water.

One radio station reported in a smooth announcer's voice that the construction of temporary housing had begun. Panic ensued at Kobe City's disaster response headquarters and the Higashi Nada Ward office. The disaster response headquarters received five hundred inquiries in just half a day, and more than fifty people showed up in person to ask about living in the temporary housing. One reason for this panic was that a rumor had begun that housing assignments would be determined on a first come, first served basis.

Several days after the Indian Ocean tsunami a rumor got started in one area that another tsunami was coming. Despite the fact that it was the middle of the night, the residents got in their cars, on their bikes, or ran on foot away from the already stricken coast.

There were similar rumors in Japan too at the time of the Great Kanto Earthquake: "Mount Fuji is about to blow"; "Chichibu Mountain Range is erupting, with ashes going up into the sky"; and "A tsunami has come and washed away all of the Kanto Plain."

Price Gouging

Roasted sweet potato, 3,000 yen ($30). 16 oz (.5 liter) bottle of water, 1,200 yen ($12). One cup ramen, 1,000 yen ($10). Two batteries, size 1, 600 yen ($6). Tank of natural gas, 800 yen ($8). These were the prices at makeshift stalls set up on street corners right after the Great Hanshin-Awaji Earthquake. Of course one would want to acquire food, water, and basic necessities amid the wreckage of a disaster. It is in these situations especially that bad people come in and try to take advantage of the situation. However, with regard to food and water, once relief supplies started to flow in, these exorbitant prices fortunately went away fairly quickly.

After the Great Hanshin-Awaji Earthquake many houses had blue sheets covering their roofs even though they had escaped being destroyed. These sheets normally cost between 2,000–3,000 yen ($20–$30), but some homeowners were being charged 200,000 yen to have the sheets installed over their roofs.

Replacing tiles on a roof also cost a lot of money. For a home whose roof was 100 square meters, the replacement cost 3,500,000 yen. The price set by the All Japan Roof Tile Contractors Federation (Zennihon Kawara Kōjigyō Renmei) for 1 square meter had been between 10,500 and 20,000 yen ($105–$200); this meant that the price being charged after the earthquake was about double. In at least one case an unscrupulous vendor tried to sell a roof tile for 5,000 yen when one *kawara* tile normally costs just 300 yen.

In another case the owners of a restaurant that had been destroyed wanted to reopen in a temporary structure as quickly as possible and asked a salvage company to come in and remove the collapsed building. The salvage company took 200,000 yen for the work but then came back the next day and demanded 800,000 yen more for a total of 1,000,000 yen ($10,000).

Someone who tried to sign a contract for an apartment offered by a friend who was a realtor suddenly found that the price had gone up by 60,000 yen to 150,000 yen on the day of the signing "at the request of the owners." Other realtors would say that there were no longer really any units available but would say that if the customer was willing to pay a little more, they might be able to find a unit. Watching the reaction of the customer, they would add that they could find a unit if a large nonrefundable or only partially refundable deposit were handed over. In this way they would dangle a unit out there to an unsuspecting customer.

In addition, large companies scooped up a lot of apartments in the northern Osaka area for their workers who had been displaced in the disaster area, and within a few weeks of the disaster there were no more units left for other people. Moreover, many unscrupulous realtors raised their monthly rents by 30,000–40,000 yen ($300–$400) at this time. They tried to argue this was just capitalism, but it is sad that they were taking advantage of people who had lost everything.

There were, however, good people that appeared during and after the disaster. For example, at one place if a motorcycle or scooter was brought in for repairs, a brand new one was sold in its place for the same price as the repairs would have been. In another case a bicycle dealer, who normally sold second-hand bicycles for about 13,000 yen, reduced his price to 9,000 yen for the victims of the disaster area. It is at times like these that humanity shows its face.

Relief Donations Fraud

According to the *Yomiuri Shimbun*,

> On February 3 (1995) the National Police Agency [Keisatsuchō] directed all prefectural headquarters [kenhonbu] to increase their

efforts to prevent rising criminal activity in the disaster area, particularly by those who are taking advantage of the situation by tricking people to donate funds that do not go to the victims or authorized organizations and by charging exorbitant fees for repairs. According to the Police Agency, in a growing number of cases criminals pretended to be representatives of the Red Cross or media and were tricking people out of donations. This has been confirmed in at least eight prefectures to date: Hokkaido, Miyagi, Fukushima, Oita, Fukuoka, Kumamoto, Kagoshima, and Okinawa.[16]

This newspaper story appeared shortly after the Great Hanshin-Awaji Earthquake. Similar things have happened since then too. More than 179 billion yen ($1.79 billion) was collected from around the country in 1995 after the earthquake. Some 6,433 people died in it, and more than 40,000 were injured. Moreover, 100,000 homes were destroyed.

The following shows the contributions received and disbursements made after some disasters in the past two decades, as well as an overview of the damages incurred at the time.

Fugendake Peak of Mt. Unzen Eruption By 1991, when the big eruption occurred, forty-four people died and 688 homes were completely destroyed. Approximately 23.2 billion yen ($232 million) was collected in donations. Of this money 9 million yen was given to families if the head of the household had died, 45 million yen was given to those whose homes had been destroyed, 740,000 yen to those who had been evacuated, and 400,000 yen to those who had lost their employment due to the affected company's laying them off. In addition, the prefecture provided additional payments out of its recovery fund: 5 million yen to assist in home rebuilding and 40,000 yen toward rent.

Hokkaido Nansei Earthquake (Okujiri Town) In total 198 people died or went missing, and 453 homes were destroyed. Some 18.7 billion yen ($187 million) was collected in donations. For the families of those who had died 3 million yen was provided. Four million was given to those whose homes had been destroyed. Business owners were given as much as 5 million yen to help keep their businesses going. Those who had been evacuated were given 50,000 yen. In addition, some 7–8 million yen was given to families who were rebuilding their homes.

Niigata-Chuetsu Earthquake Forty-eight people died, and 3,173 homes were destroyed. Some 36.2 billion yen ($362 million) was collected. Two hundred thousand yen was paid to families who had lost someone and 100,000 yen to those who had been injured. Two million was paid to families whose homes had been destroyed and 1 million to those whose homes had sustained substantial damage. In addition, 250,000 yen was given to those whose homes had been less than half destroyed, and 50,000 yen was given to those who had some sort of damage.

Fukuoka Earthquake It may be because large-scale disasters had been occurring one after the other, but by the end of May 2005 only 835 million yen ($8.35 million) had been collected, which amounted to less than 3 percent of the money gathered after the Niigata-Chuetsu Earthquake the previous fall.

The money donations came from people all around the country and from public coffers, comprised of taxpayers' money. And yet there were those who, sadly, tried to profit from the disasters.

"Be careful of donation scams. Make sure before you send money." This warning appears on the website of a list of organizations receiving donations. It is disheartening to see this warning when people want to give and help out. On the website is a list of local governments, newspapers, and television stations and a description of the organizations receiving donations and their account information for electronically sending money.

One activity that has become more common is the linking of online advertisers with donations. When you click on the advertiser or sponsor of a site, a certain amount of money, perhaps 1 yen or more, is supposedly sent to an organization identified as the recipient of the funds. This is a carefree way that does not cost one money to give. However, this manner of donations does not really seem to be in line with the true sense of charitable "giving." It is impersonal and even commercial. It seems just to be an easy way to collect money.

In light of the potential for misuse of donations and actual fraudulent ways money has been gathered, some warnings are being placed on the Internet and in other public locations. Some of the warnings are as follows:

> There are a number of scandals in which the names of donation organizations are being fraudulently used.
>
> The Niigata-Chuetsu Earthquake Response Headquarters is not soliciting donations by postcard or email.
>
> A donation scandal is emerging with the Niigata-Chuetsu Earthquake whereby a person pretending to be a city employee is soliciting donations.
>
> We have learned that a group is soliciting donations by pretending to be the Japan Red Cross Society and sending postcards to individuals' homes.
>
> The Japan Red Cross is warning people that it does not go to one's home or solicit donations by letter or postcard.
>
> I was walking around and overhead some so-called volunteers out there who were collecting money and talking among themselves. "How much did you collect?" one asked. The other answered, "About 10,000 yen. I think I'll get a bike tomorrow."[17]

As mentioned, such comments were listed on websites to warn people against making donations without checking into the recipient organizations.

Several months after the March 20, 2005, Fukuoka Earthquake, some suspicious fliers turned up in Ichikawa City, Chiba Prefecture, calling upon people to make donations. Authorities were able to close the account that had been established to accept donations.

A television show did an investigative report on organizations soliciting donations suspiciously in July 2005. The show was called "Detailed Pursuit! Mysterious Street Donations" (Tettei tsuiseki! Nazo no gaitō bokin) and went after some of these suspicious organizations. In one case an organization donated 450,000 yen—or 10 percent of the money it had collected—but used the remainder for "operating expenses."

Any group can go out and collect donations on the street as long it files for permission with the police to use the streets or sidewalks. It is probably necessary to establish more legal procedures to make it tougher to take advantage of people.

After the May 2005 accident when a JR West (JR Nishi) train derailed and killed dozens of people in Amagasaki City, Hyogo Prefecture, some people pretended to have been passengers on the train in order to collect compensation from JR.

Irresponsible Media

I have an email dated October 28, 2004, that says, "Help! Ojiya City, Niigata Prefecture." It was an appeal from a woman who went to work as a volunteer at an evacuation shelter after the Niigata-Chuetsu Earthquake. It reads as follows:

> I am here helping out at the Ojiya City Hall and nearby elementary school, delivering relief supplies and helping prepare meals. The situation here is still in confusion. We do not have enough help here, that is for sure. Despite this, some fifty reporters have come and set themselves up here at the Ojiya city offices. Unbelievably, they have parked right in front of the city offices, so relief supplies must be carried a much farther distance as the delivery trucks have to park further away. The volunteers and staff have worked hard to carry everything inside. The god-damned reporters just watch and do not lend a hand. And then the reporters shove their microphones in the faces of the victims of the disaster, people who are already mentally and physically exhausted over what they have been through. Twenty-four hours a day, the media are here with the cameras rolling. I cannot understand at all what they are thinking. We are running out of adult diapers, but we have enough baby diapers. We cannot use the bathrooms and do not have underwear to change into. Panty liners are very valuable in that sense. However, they have long been sold out. Please call Procter and Gamble, Kao, Nepia, the makers of panty liners, and tell them about the situation here. It is very cold here at night. There are not enough heating pads, so the elderly are having a very difficult time. I think it is the job of the media to

tell these stories and get this information and these requests out. [Prime Minister] Koizumi [Junichiro] is supposed to visit Ojiya Elementary School now, so the number of media here has swelled considerably. We were told that his coming is affecting the delivery of some blankets and other relief supplies, and we are being told to wait until he leaves. Why is he coming in the first place? This morning some politicians visited the elementary school as well. When they asked to use the restrooms, they were brought to the port-a-johns but apparently expressed revulsion at having to use them. What is wrong with this country when the elected leaders don't even understand the misery that the victims of disasters, their fellow countrymen, have to live with?[18]

The email continued, "We cannot rely on or trust the media. They are in the way and preventing the provision of assistance here. Their presence and actions are increasing the concerns and worries of the victims of the disaster. Please protest against their manner of reporting and behavior. It is really bad here."

A lot of helicopters, most of them from the media, flew over the disaster area at the time of the Great Hanshin-Awaji Earthquake. They caused the voices of those trapped underneath the rubble to be drowned out, and they were a huge hindrance to the rescue efforts. In addition, the media, in the name of reporting, would audaciously force their way into access-restricted areas with their cars and motorcycles and occupy precious parking spaces at city and ward offices that were also serving as command centers and evacuation shelters. The media also unreservedly stuck their microphones in the faces of families who had lost loved ones or their homes, belongings, and everything. In doing so, the media brought upon themselves the ire of many.

Of course to the reporters behaving in this way, it was their job. The media are a particularly competitive industry, and it is dog eat dog. In part thanks to the media, a lot of people from around Japan sent relief supplies, donated money, and went to the disaster area as volunteers.

At the time of the Niigata-Chuetsu Earthquake a survey was taken to see what form of media was most useful in getting out information about the disaster during the first week. Respondents answered as follows: radio (90.0 percent), newspapers (57.8 percent), television (56.9 percent), fliers at evacuation shelters (19.9 percent), city hall–produced newsletters, public announcements on loudspeakers, and other sources of information (varies between 1 and 8 percent). In light of these results, it is very clear that the media's role, when compared to that of public sources of information, is quite large.

It goes without saying that it is important to gather and document the many things that are happening for future reference, but at least in the middle of a large disaster, when immediately saving lives and bringing relief is essential, the media outlets should put aside their competition, avoid duplication, and share their information to lessen the impact on affected communities and services. Is this too much to ask?

Even if the information is shared, it does not mean that the stories have to be all the same. The producers of television shows and the writers and editors of newspapers could introduce the information in their own ways. What is important is that the true sense of what has happened in the disaster is introduced and that the feelings of the people in the disaster areas are taken into consideration. What certainly is not acceptable is that hordes of reporters descend on a disaster area, act insensitively toward the suffering around them, and walk around the disaster area at will looking for stories among the victims.

One of the important roles of the mass media is the daily edification of readers and viewers. If the residents in the areas that were affected by the Indian Ocean tsunami had had a better grasp of the danger presented by the earthquake and subsequent tsunami, the number of victims would have been much fewer.

However, even in the earthquake country that Japan is, while the public is of course affected by the individual dramas of disaster victims, at least one reporter questions just how closely the subscribers of newspapers actually read the stories. This reporter says he can only continue to tell the stories of the victims and report on newly occurred disasters, thereby informing the readership of the danger of earthquakes.

Natural disasters are unavoidable. One of the important roles of the media is to truthfully report on disasters and suggest the proper way to deal with them.

Trauma

People who have lost family members or their homes in a large-scale disaster or who have been badly injured themselves often suffer from post-traumatic stress disorder, or PTSD. Those that have PTSD may have trouble sleeping or lose their appetites or, in more serious cases, suddenly start crying or screaming as they remember something about the tragedy they experienced and begin to panic. Some even go into bouts of depression. According to a nationwide study conducted in the United States about PTSD cases in disasters, 5 percent of men and 10 percent of women get PTSD. In recent cases of massive accidents or school shootings it has been common to have mental health counselors on the scene.

At the time of the Great Hanshin-Awaji Earthquake as well, a mental health care support office was established within the health centers of particularly hard hit areas of Kobe City. Psychologists, nurses, and mental health counselors from all around the country volunteered and were dispatched there to assist.

The simplest form of treatment is for a victim to talk about the problem rather than keeping it covered up inside. By talking about one's sadness and sharing one's difficult experiences, it is believed that one discovers that he or she is not alone and will find the confidence one day to overcome the problem.

In the case of large disasters, the effects are not temporary but last a while. For those that lost family members, their homes, or their jobs, their suffering will continue. Some people have to stay in evacuation shelters before they are able to move into temporary housing. Often the temporary housing is located far from the neighborhoods with which they are familiar. After the Great Hanshin-Awaji Earthquake some 40 percent of those who moved into temporary housing were elderly, over sixty-five years old. Half of those people, moreover, were either widowed or otherwise by themselves. More than 250 people died alone and went undiscovered for a while, and 70 percent of them were males. Following the Niigata-Chuetsu Earthquake, in order to prevent such incidents, known as "dying alone" (*kodokushi*), temporary housing units were built within the existing neighborhoods.

After a large-scale disaster people who have survived might gradually develop psychological issues. It would be a shame if they died in this way after having survived a horrific natural disaster.

CHAPTER 3

Trench-Type Megaquakes

Why Trench-Type Earthquakes Are a Threat

A ferocious mass of water pushes in from the coastline abruptly. Rubble; what used to be houses, buildings, stores, post offices, schools, train stations, trees, cars, bicycles; and people are engulfed; murky water flows into the roads, residents screaming in panic and running wildly to escape. Wreckage and rubble crushed by a massive force lay spread over the surface. A fishing vessel lies on its side, far inland from the coast. A car, having penetrated through the walls of a house, is visible. People are trapped within the rubble. Mothers are crying out for help, carrying their children covered in mud. These are images that have recreated the horror and powerful force of tsunamis across the globe. One person who was swallowed up by a tsunami but miraculously survived later said, "It was as if I were in a washing machine, spinning with rubble and mud."

The date was December 26, 2004. A magnitude 9.0 megaquake struck off the coast of Indonesia's western province, Sumatra Island. This earthquake had 1,600 times the energy of the Great Hanshin-Awaji Earthquake, which struck off the coast of southern Hyogo Prefecture and had a magnitude of 7.3.

The tsunami following the earthquake struck Indonesia's province of Aceh and neighboring nations along the Indian Ocean coastline — Sri Lanka, India, Thailand, and Malaysia. The tsunami left over 220,000 people dead or missing and over 5 million refugees. The earthquake and tsunami of Sumatra became one of the most devastating disasters in recorded history.

This tsunami knocked the roofs off of buildings with waves that were five meters high and washed away the foundations of railway lines, leaving the rails twisted and damaged trains on their sides. Hundreds of boats were washed ashore, and large trees were stuck on top of electrical poles. These were some of the images we frequently saw after the disaster.

There were also many deaths attributed to people attempting to escape the tsunami by buses or trains that were swallowed up by the tidal wave. The tsunami's instantaneous pressure at the time was calculated at eighteen tons per square meter. This pressure is equivalent to the impact of a four-ton truck traveling at 30–40 km/h. This energy can easily knock down average concrete-block walls, electrical poles, wooden buildings, etc., as we saw in the images from 2004 (and later from Japan in March 2011).

On December 21, 1946, around 4:30 a.m., the tide withdrew rapidly from the coastline of Tanabe City, Wakayama Prefecture. Soon after, a giant tidal wave forced its way onto land with a horrific roar. This tsunami was caused by the Showa Nankai Earthquake (Shōwa Nankai Jishin).[1] Within ten minutes all of the city's coastlines, spread across ten kilometers, were crushed by a tsunami of four to five meters. A six-meter tsunami was also recorded making its way within the city. Some 269 went dead or missing in Wakayama Prefecture as a result of this tsunami. The overall damage from the earthquake was 1,330 deaths, 11,591 homes destroyed, and 1,451 homes washed away by the tsunami.

The Tonankai Earthquake had struck two years earlier, in 1944, resulting in 1,223 deaths and missing persons and the complete destruction of 17,599 houses.[2]

In preparing for another Tonankai or Nankai earthquake scenario, the government's Central Disaster Management Council (introduced in chapter 1 and described in more detail in chapter 6) published its estimates of the likely damage in 2003. The estimated death toll for Wakayama Prefecture would be 5,100 according to the council's report.[3]

Although the threat from earthquakes and tsunamis is frequently discussed, it still seems that to most people such a threat is just something to watch on television and does not really affect them. Occasionally earthquake warning messages appear on the top, bottom, or sides of the television screen, but most people disregard them unless they actually feel a quake. The earthquake warnings and information are followed by tsunami warnings. "There are no threats of a tsunami from this earthquake," is the usual televised warning. Before broadcasting the warnings, the Meteorological Agency groups the tsunamis into the following categories, according to the forecasted height of the tsunami: giant tsunami, or ōtsunami (three meters, four meters, six meters, eight meters, ten meters+); tsunami (1–2 meters); and tsunami warning, or tsunami chui (0–0.5 meters).

The largest tsunamis do not always move toward the coastline facing the earthquake's epicenter.[4] The height of the tsunami varies according to the shape of the coastline and the topography of the ocean's bottom.

Some topographic examples that enable tsunamis to increase in height are the following: the tip of a cape, coastlines with shallows that extend outward, the back of a cape's wraparound, and bays shaped in a "V." These geographic features allow the energy from the tsunami to concentrate on one point, making the tsunami even larger. Tsunamis may grow multifold or exponentially in tight bays or other areas.[5]

Tsunamis move toward land after a strong pull of the tide. This rapid water movement can pull people in and drown them in water less than one meter deep. The destructive force of the tsunami destroys everything in its path—trees, boulders, cars, houses, and furniture; nothing on land is safe in the path of a tsunami. It is noteworthy that not all tsunami deaths are caused by drowning. Many are from the intense water pressure crushing the human body. Tsunami survivors suffer many bruises and lacerations all over their bodies.

In Japan there are many highways that run along the coastline. It is nice to drive and gaze at the ocean, but at times it can be life threatening.

Tsunamis travel faster over waters with a deep ocean floor. At a water depth of 4,000 meters, the tsunami travels at 700 km/h, and near the continental shelf, with a depth of 200 meters, the tsunami travels at 160 km/h toward land. On land the tsunami can travel up to 30 km/h, a speed that humans cannot outrun.

In Japan it is now possible to somewhat accurately forecast tsunamis—namely, it is possible to predict (among other things) a tsunami's occurrence, expected arrival time, and average height of the wave. However, a forecast lacks accurate information on how a tsunami will hit each specific location and how it will force its way inland. Forecasts, in other words, are sometimes wrong altogether about heights and the degree of actual destruction.

Currently throughout Japan local governments make their own tsunami hazard maps. However, these hazard maps list only the regions that will be assumed to be flooded and the expected water levels cause by the tidal wave. As we have learned from the giant tsunami off of Indonesia, tsunamis are not simply an increase in water levels. The water movement causes enormous energy to head toward land. The hazard maps require information regarding each region's topography, the population's age and composition, and other demographics, as well as the locations of evacuation routes and refuge sites. Detailed information on the tsunami and the cooperation of the residents are key to a successful evacuation. It is impossible to create a realistic evacuation scenario employing disaster prevention and reduction measures without the residents' cooperation and awareness about the dangers of earthquakes and tsunamis.

History Speaks

"It wouldn't be surprising if it happened again." Those words are constantly on the minds of those who speak of the Tokai earthquake scenario. The statement is strongly supported by statistical evidence based on the history of earthquake occurrences. According to ancient historical documents, giant earthquakes and tsunamis occur periodically in the region.

The mechanism of "trench-type" earthquakes and tsunamis also adds an element of truth to the historical documents. Continental plates that have been pressed together and bending for a long time will spring up when they are no longer able to withstand the pressure. These types of plate-shifting activity occur regularly within

Earth. This simple explanation is easy for everyone to understand and has a great persuasive power.

Tsunamis are created from a plate's upward spring, caused by trench-type earthquakes. The earthquake causes the ocean surface to either swell or subside, creating a massive water movement, which in turn becomes a tsunami.

The earthquake off of the coast of Sumatra was a trench-type earthquake caused by the upspring of Indo-Australian Plate, which slips under the Eurasian Plate. Sumatra's trench-type earthquake had the same mechanism as that of the Tokai, Tonankai, and Nankai earthquake scenarios. The difference between Indonesia's and Japan's trench-type earthquakes is the length of the fault lines. Even if all three types of earthquakes were to occur in Japan, the fault line is six hundred kilometers long, but the Indonesian earthquake moved one thousand kilometers, north to south, on the fault line. The giant tsunami was caused by the upspring movement of the fault spreading across one thousand kilometers.

Four large plates collide with each other near the Japanese archipelago: the Eurasian, North American, Pacific, and Philippine Sea Plates. The borderlines where the plates meet is a trench called a trough. The Suruga Trough stretches from east Suruga Bay to offshore Enshunan (near Aichi Prefecture). To the west of the Suruga Trough is the Nankai Trough.

The Tokai, Tonankai, and Nankai earthquake scenarios all occur on the borderlines where the Eurasian Plate and the Philippine Sea Plate meet. The earthquakes that occur in the Suruga Trough (from off Shizuoka Prefecture to off Hamanako) are the Tokai types. Earthquakes that occur in the Nankai Trough (from off Hamanako to off Shiosaki on the Kii Peninsula) are the Tonankai types. The earthquakes with epicenters from Shiosaki to Cape Ashizuri are the Nankai types. For all three types of earthquakes the Philippine Sea Plate is pushing into the Eurasian Plate slipping underneath it. The Eurasian Plate becomes contorted as time passes, and when the plate cannot withstand the pressure, it springs up, creating a giant trench-type earthquake. From the Hakuho Earthquake (684) through the Nankai Earthquake (1946), there have been twelve major earthquakes originating from the Suruga and Nankai Troughs. Historically the Tokai, Tonankai, and Nankai earthquake scenarios have occurred in order from the east or simultaneously. The interval of these occurrences is between 90 and 150 years.[6] The following lists those earthquakes and tsunamis, the names given to them, and the areas affected by them.

1498—Meio Earthquake (magnitude 8.6; Tokai, Tonankai)
Tsunami death toll: Suruga—26,000; Ise (Mie Prefecture)—15,000
1605—Keicho Earthquake (magnitude 7.9; Tonankai, Nankai)
Tsunami struck a wide range of regions from Chiba Prefecture to the Kyushu region. Total death toll: 2,500
1707—Hoei Earthquake (magnitude 8.4; Tokai, Tonankai, Nankai)
Japan's largest earthquake (to date, prior to the March 2011 disaster). The plates offshore of Tokai and plates offshore of Shikoku simultaneously shifted. Total death toll: 20,000
1854—Ansei Tokai Earthquake (magnitude 8.4; Tokai, Tonankai)
Ansei Nankai Earthquake (magnitude 8.4; Nankai)
The Ansei Nankai Earthquake occurred thirty-two hours after the Ansei Tokai Earthquake. The tsunami caused by the Ansei Tokai Earthquake struck the Enshunan and Suruga Bay, killing 2,000–3,000 people. The tsunami caused by the Ansei Nankai Earthquake struck the Kii Peninsula and the Shikoku region, killing several thousand people.
1944—Tonankai Earthquake (magnitude 8.0; Tonankai)
1946—Nankai Earthquake (magnitude 8.1; Nankai)
The two major earthquakes occurred within two years of each other. The tsunami from the Tonankai Earthquake struck the Izu Peninsula and Kii Peninsula, killing 1,233 people. The Nankai Earthquake's tsunami struck from Shizuoka Prefecture to Kyushu, killing 1,350 people.

When we compare the earthquakes over time, it is evident that the earthquakes occur after the energy stored within the earth's crust is released all at once. There is also a high possibility for the

Tokai, Tonankai, and Nankai types of earthquakes to occur one after the other.

The Tokai and Tonankai types of earthquake struck almost simultaneously during the Ansei Tokai Earthquake of 1854, causing the plate from Suruga Bay to the Kii Peninsula to shift. This means that the plate from the Tokai earthquake shifted without releasing any energy. About 150 years have passed since the last Tokai-type earthquake, and the confidence behind the statement that "It will happen again" comes from this historical evidence.

Actual observations and scientific calculations also predict that another Tokai-type earthquake is likely to occur. However, even the average person without any prior knowledge of such earthquakes can easily understand and be persuaded when the historical timeline is presented. However, it is sad to say that our strongest evidence of another earthquake striking is simply based on old, historical documents and not on calculations using high-tech equipment or supercomputers.

Why does the Tokai earthquake scenario receive all of this special attention? The Tokai-type earthquake is the only scenario that is considered to be "predictable." Using this predictability as a basis, the Large-Scale Earthquake Special Measures Law (Daikibo Jishin Taisaku Tokubetsu Sochihō), described in greater detail in chapter 6, was passed in 1978. Under this law if the government were to announce an earthquake warning, civilian life could be restricted to martial law–like conditions.

Damage Estimates for the Tokai Earthquake Scenario
by the Central Disaster Management Council

Three important conditions are predicted for the next giant trench-type earthquake:

1. A Tokai earthquake will occur by itself, with the energy left behind from the last earthquake.
2. Tonankai and Nankai earthquakes will occur either with some slight delay from each other or simultaneously.
3. All three earthquakes will occur simultaneously.

Of the three conditions the third would obviously have the most devastating effect. On March 3, 2003, the Central Disaster Management Council's Tokai Earthquake Measures Experts Committee (Tōkai Jishin Taisaku Senmonkai) published a document concerning the estimated damage resulting from the next Tokai earthquake. The committee estimated the next Tokai earthquake to be within the range of magnitude 8.0. The estimated damage report also contained a wide range of hypothesized situations:

Estimated time of occurrence
Winter, 5:00 a.m.; fall, 12:00 p.m.; winter, 6:00 p.m.

Estimated tsunami
Situation where residents' awareness about dangers of tsunami is high; situation where residents' awareness is low; situation where floodgates function poorly

Estimated fires
Wind speed of three meters and wind speed of fifteen meters

Earthquake prediction information
Earthquake happens without prior warning; earthquake happens with a warning

The estimated damage is calculated by combining the different factors mentioned above, but it is extremely complicated. In reality it would be hard for a person with no training to understand.

It is estimated that the situation in which an earthquake strikes at 5:00 a.m. and without any earthquake warning will have the most casualties—around 9,200 dead and 15,000 injured. However, if an earthquake warning is issued, the death toll and number of injuries will be greatly reduced—to 2,300 and 4,000 respectively.[7]

It is estimated that building damages will be greatest if an earthquake strikes at 6:00 p.m., destroying 460,000 homes. Further, it is estimated that 170,000 buildings will be damaged by the initial shaking, 6,800 by the tsunami, 26,000 by water damage, and 250,000 by fires. If warnings are issued prior to the earthquake, the spread of fires can be prevented, and fire damage can be reduced to 7,600 structures.

It is estimated that the destruction of buildings and water/electricity/gas utility infrastructures from the earthquake will have a direct economic damage of 26 trillion yen ($260 billion). Indirect economic effects caused by the shutdown of factories, traffic network damages, etc., will reach an estimated 11 trillion yen ($110 billion). The total economic damage is estimated at 37 trillion yen ($370 billion).[8] However, the estimated economic damage is calculated on the assumption that earthquake warnings were not issued. If earthquake warnings were issued, the total economic damage could be reduced by 6 trillion yen, making the total of damage 31 trillion yen ($310 billion). The committee stated that even a 6 trillion yen reduction in the total economic damage would have a significant effect overall.

It is also estimated that the number of evacuees will reach 20 million and that a further 50 million more refugees will be affected by the limited access to essentials such as gas, water, and electricity.

It is interesting to note that official documents estimate that the highest cause of death will be the crushing of people in collapsed homes. Such an estimate is partly based on past experiences of giant earthquakes—namely, the Great Hanshin-Awaji Earthquake, in which 80 percent of the deaths occurred in collapsed structures—and it was the easiest assumption to make. However, the measures of disasters in modern metropolises cannot be based on simple assumptions. As noted, the cities' layout, scale, and time of occurrence of an earthquake have a significant effect on the amount of damage.

For instance, what if a Tokai earthquake were to occur during a summer afternoon? At least one hundred thousand people would probably be enjoying their leisure time at the beaches at Shonan, south of Tokyo. There are already traffic jams caused by all of the beachgoers along the coastal highway on normal summer days and especially on the weekends. What would happen if a tsunami similar to the Indonesian one were to strike a place like Shonan with all the beachgoers there? Few would be able to escape.

If a Tokai earthquake were to occur, a tsunami would greatly complicate the situation; there would be damage to the Shinkansen and other railway lines, underground shopping malls and arcades, boats docked at wharves, and industrial complexes that line the coast.

The Central Disaster Management Council also published a damage assessment report (updated after the March 11 disaster) that takes into consideration the simultaneous occurrence of a Tonankai and a Nankai earthquake. In the worst case (according to the earlier version of the report), it was estimated that the death toll would reach over 25,000, caused by collapsed buildings, a tsunami, and fires across thirteen prefectures (Chubu region to Kyushu region). This estimate was based on the assumption that the earthquake occurred at 5:00 a.m., the wind speed was 15 m/h, the floodgates were unable to close, and the evacuation plan was unclear and poorly understood by local residents. Some 29,000 people would suffer serious injuries, and over 39,300 would require some sort of rescue/aid.

It was estimated that the loss of buildings from the initial quake, fire, and tsunami would be greatest if the earthquake struck at 6:00 p.m. with a wind speed of 15 m/h. It was estimated that 31,600 buildings would be destroyed if those conditions were met. Within a week of the initial earthquake, the refugee count would likely reach over 4.4 million. However, even this estimated damage assessment could not accurately consider all the unknown factors.

The worst-case scenario is a simultaneous occurrence of Tokai, Tonankai, and Nankai earthquakes. Looking back in history, we see that the three earthquakes occurred simultaneously in the 1707 Hoei Earthquake and the 1854 Ansei earthquakes. The Central Disaster Management Council has estimated that should all three earthquakes occur at once, they would be a magnitude 7.8. The council has also estimated the damage for such a scenario.

At the center of the earthquake—the Pacific coast from the west up to the Kanto region—in the worst case according to the report at the time, it was estimated that 960,000 buildings would be obliterated by the earthquake, tsunami, and following fires. If the earthquake occurred at 5:00 a.m., 12,200 deaths would be expected from structural collapses, 12,700 from the tsunami, and 3,500 from fires and landslides.

The economic damage was also predicted to be extremely large. Damaged and destroyed buildings and infrastructures that support water, gas, and other lifelines would account for 40–60 trillion yen in direct damage ($400–600 billion). Indirect damage was expected to be around 13–21 trillion yen ($130–210 billion), caused by discontinued production at factories and a suspension of the transportation network. At most, the death toll was expected to reach just over 28,000, and the economic loss/damage would reach 81 trillion yen.

If a Tokai earthquake does not strike within the next ten years, the possibility of Tokai, Tonankai, and Nankai earthquakes striking simultaneously increases. The Central Disaster Management Council also acknowledges the dangers of a magnitude 7 inland earthquake striking Tokyo. If all four of these earthquakes were to occur simultaneously, the estimated economic loss/damage would be expected to reach over 300 trillion yen ($3 trillion), which is equivalent to four times the national budget. Such a scenario poses a real threat to the survival of Japan as a nation.

The Reliability and Ability of Citizens to Respond to Earthquake Warnings

It is speculated that the pre-slip, which preludes an earthquake, is observable for a Tokai earthquake, reaffirming the possibility of predicting an earthquake. Warnings of the earthquake will be issued in stages through the observation of the pre-slip.

Since January 2004 a new information system that integrates an objective evaluation standard for a Tokai earthquake has been established. Prior to the new system, when the strain gauge set up specifically to monitor a Tokai earthquake sensed abnormal activity, a six-member panel met to discuss the measures to take. Excerpts from a pamphlet the Cabinet Office and Meteorological Agency issued in 2004, titled "The Prediction and Disaster Measures for a Tokai Earthquake—How to Properly Use 'Information on the Observation of a Tokai Earthquake,'" follows.[9]

"Tokai Earthquake Observation Information"

Information on the observation of a Tokai earthquake will be issued when a situation cannot be immediately evaluated based on the pre-slip phenomenon of a Tokai earthquake. (That is, at least one strain gauge observes a significant change or remarkable seismic activity cannot be immediately identified as having any relation with a Tokai earthquake.) There are no particular disaster prevention measures. The government and local authorities assessing the information and the situation will communicate. Residents should carry on with their daily lives but pay close attention to information on television, radio, etc.

"Tokai Earthquake Warning Information"

Warning information is issued when a prelude phenomenon to a Tokai earthquake is observed and a Tokai earthquake is deemed possible. (That is, at least two strain gauges at different locations observe significant changes and it is deemed possible that the changes were caused by the prelude phenomenon.) Take the following precautionary measures for disaster prevention to prepare for a Tokai earthquake. Secure the safety of infants and students and take measures to send them home. Prepare the dispatch of rescue teams, emergency teams, fire departments, and medical personnel. A meeting will be held by the Meteorological Agency to reevaluate the situation and the possibility that it is leading to a Tokai earthquake. Residents should pay careful attention to the information on television, radio, etc. When necessary, follow the evacuation plan announced by the government and local authorities.

"Tokai Earthquake Imminent Information"

Imminent information is issued when it is predicted that a Tokai earthquake is likely to occur. (That is, more than three strain gauges observe a significant change and it is acknowledged that the pre-slip is the cause.) A "Warning Announcement" will be issued. Earthquake disaster security headquarters will be established. The evacuation of residents and road closures will take place in regions in danger of a tsunami and landslides. Department stores will be closed immediately in those regions. Residents should pay close attention to information on television, radio, etc. Follow the evacuation instructions/disaster prevention plans provided by local authorities, etc.

According to this new information system, when the Meteorological Agency detects unusual activity, it will first issue "Tokai

Earthquake Observation Information." If unusual activity is detected at two different locations, "Tokai Earthquake Warning Information" will be issued. If unusual activity is detected at three or more locations, "Tokai Earthquake Imminent Information" will be issued. This system is based on standards that are quite objective compared to the prior system, which relied on the subjective opinions of scientists. However, there is no guarantee that the stages that are seen as preludes to a Tokai earthquake will occur smoothly and that the evacuation of residents will take place with enough time to spare. This is as an example of the expression "Easier said than done."

What if one day, out of nowhere, a "Warning Announcement" were issued? If it was issued on a weekday afternoon, mothers would hurry to the schools to pick up their children, and fathers would take some sort of action to protect their families. People would quickly disappear from department stores, underground shopping arcades, movie theaters, etc. From there a rush of people would head to stores that were still open to purchase food and emergency supplies and to banks to draw out cash. Employees of the stores would probably want to head home as well. Everybody would rush to their home-bound train stations, but the trains would not be running. The highways would be backed up with cars full of people rushing to get home or evacuate to a safer place. In other words, there would be mass chaos.

People who were able to return home would all gather around the television to get news of the earthquake. Or they would sit there waiting for the "Warning Announcement" to clear. Can you imagine the feelings they would experience at this time? Many people would also have left for designated evacuation sites.

If the "Warning Announcement" were extended, people would get ill after a while due to worry and anxiety over a long period. The hospitals, however, would no longer be accepting out-patients. The roads would all be backed up with people trying to evacuate to safer ground.

It is estimated that the economic losses from one day after the issue of the "Warning Announcement" would be around 2 billion yen ($20 million). Some researchers have estimated that economic losses might reach 3.5 billion yen per day ($35 million).

In the pamphlet some disclaimers state the following: "In a situation when the pre-slip occurs rapidly or the pre-slip is of small scale, information regarding the earthquake might not be available"; "Technology has been progressing every year to be able to predict a Tokai earthquake. However, at the present stage, while it sometimes may be possible to issue a warning for a Tokai earthquake, there are other times when it won't be possible. It is important to be prepared in case an earthquake should occur"; and "Verify your home's earthquake resistance," "Secure your furniture," "Stock up on food and beverages," and "Participate in your local evacuation drills." It makes one want to ask if the authorities can actually predict an earthquake or not. If it is possible to predict an earthquake, will the warning come ten minutes before, an hour before, or one day before? The time frame for when a warning will be issued is not made clear in the pamphlet. I doubt I am the only one who is frustrated with this pamphlet, which seems to avoid precision.

As stated above, a movement that precedes the earthquake is called a "pre-slip" and is the indicator for a warning announcement to be issued. In the case of a Tokai earthquake, the slow movement of the pre-slip is the indicator before the plate's full-scale movement. This pre-slip theory, with some possibilities, has come to be debated more among earthquake researchers in recent years.

The pre-slip phenomenon is supported by a ground level measurement that assesses the vertical movement of the ground soil; such a measurement was conducted near Kakegawa City, Shizuoka Prefecture, during the December 7,1944, Tokai earthquake. Two days prior to the earthquake ground movement was observed, and the day of the earthquake there was a ground movement of 5 mm. This movement is the phenomenon called the pre-slip. If a pre-slip can be observed beforehand, the earthquake can be predicted. Seismic observation equipment was placed throughout Japan after it was proven that predicting earthquakes was possible.

However, there have been no cases of pre-slip observations prior to big earthquakes since the 1944 Tokai earthquake. A pre-slip was not detected during the 2003 Tokachi Earthquake, a large trench-type earthquake with a magnitude 8.0. Similarly in the September

2004 series of earthquakes that shook the Kii Peninsula, the first earthquake's epicenter was determined to be at a depth of only ten kilometers with a magnitude 6.9, and the second earthquake, which struck soon after, packed a magnitude 7.3. However, even though these two were trench-type earthquakes, it was not possible to predict them because the pre-slip phenomenon was not detected in either case.

Are the Nuclear Reactors Safe?

Tokai earthquakes cannot be discussed without mentioning the nuclear reactors. Chubu Electric's Hamaoka Nuclear Power Plant (Hamaoka Genshiryoku Hatusdensho) in Shizuoka Prefecture stands directly above the presumed epicenter of a Tokai earthquake. What would happen if a magnitude 8.0 earthquake hit this region? (Indeed this became the biggest question facing Japan after the March 11 disaster.)

Let's imagine a worst-case scenario. Suppose that the core cooling system for the nuclear reactor became dysfunctional from the quake. On top of that, the emergency core reactor shutdown system malfunctioned. Nuclear reactions would advance within the core reactor, and uranium used for fuel would begin to melt. This is the so-called meltdown of a nuclear power plant.

Uranium that has reached high temperatures would melt the reactor pressure vessel, which in turn would collapse into the nuclear core containment vessel. The Hamaoka Nuclear Power Plant is a boiling-water nuclear reactor, which has a pressure suppression pool at the bottom. If the reactor pressure vessel collapsed into the containment vessel, it would result in a vapor explosion. The explosion would damage parts of the reactor pressure vessel and the nuclear reactor containment vessel. Cracks in the pipeline caused by the explosion would allow vapors that contain radioactive particles to be released throughout the nuclear reactor facility. (This is essentially the way in which the Fukushima Nuclear Power Plant disaster happened after the March 11 earthquake and tsunami.)

Further, if the nuclear power plant's facilities were destroyed by the earthquake and exploded, it would mean radioactive particles would be released into the atmosphere. If this were to happen, not only would nearby cities be contaminated, but it could even affect Tokyo, depending on the wind direction. Even if there were no major damage to the nuclear reactor itself, if any of the pipelines in the facility were to burst due to high heat, radioactive particles would be sent into the atmosphere. And then there would be a strong possibility leading to the following scenario, introduced by the *Asahi Shimbun*:

> If there were to be an accident at Hamaoka Nuclear Power Plant, how many people would be exposed to radioactivity? Based on a program developed by the late Seo Ken, a research assistant at Kyoto University Research Reactor Institute [Kyōto Daigaku Genshiro Jikkensho], Koide Hiroaki, another research assistant at the same laboratory, calculated the estimated number of people exposed. The working assumption was that Hamaoka's Reactor No. 2 (840,000 kilowatts), a reactor pressure vessel, exploded and released large amounts of radioactive particles into the atmosphere. The population in the area was based on the 2000 census, and it was assumed that every resident had evacuated the area within one week of the accident. If the wind was blowing toward Nagoya City (Aichi Prefecture), 47,000 people would die from immediate radiation poisoning, and 330,000 people would die later from cancer caused by radiation in Aichi Prefecture, with the total death toll estimated to reach at least 950,000. If the wind direction was toward Tokyo, the total death toll was estimated to reach 1.76 million. However, this simulation does not take into account the possibility that the nuclear power plant accident and an earthquake occurred simultaneously. If the roads have been destroyed due to the earthquake, it would make it impossible for rescue teams to go in and would make it difficult to take emergency measures. Similarly evacuees would not be able to leave easily and thus would be unable to evade the high-density radiation that would be closing in on them. Moreover, fearing radiation poisoning, rescue workers would find it difficult to assist. Such a situation is called the "Nuclear Plant Disaster" scenario.

It is unscientific to claim that this situation is "highly unlikely and possibilities of it are low" without any evidence. Koide says that a debate is necessary to assess the amount of damage and determine the likelihood of such a situation.[10]

Nuclear reactor facilities are designed and built according to the "Earthquake Resistant Design Examination Guidelines Regarding Nuclear Power Reactor Facilities" (Hatsudenyō Genshiro Shisetsu ni Kansuru Taishin Sekkei Shinsa Shishin), established in 1981. In essence nuclear power plants are to be built on the following basic principles: "Construct nuclear power plants on solid foundations, avoiding building directly above active faults and ensuring that the plants will be able to resist an earthquake from a nearby fault" and that they will "be able to resist a magnitude 6.5 direct-hit earthquake."[11]

Nevertheless, it is clear that Chubu Electric's Hamaoka Nuclear Power Plant is built within the presumed epicenter of a Tokai earthquake. The presumed epicenter has a rectangular shape, eleven kilometers long and seventy kilometers wide. There are no active faults directly below the Hamaoka Nuclear Power Plant, but it is built over an earthquake fault. In response, the Hamaoka Nuclear Power Plant has stated that all of its vital facilities are constructed with rigid structures and that there are no problems in its earthquake safety measures.

In general nuclear power plants are designed to be three times more resistant to earthquakes than ordinary buildings under the Construction Standards Act (Kensetsu Kijunhō) or stronger than any known earthquake to affect the area in which they are built.

Hamaoka Reactors Nos. 1 and 2 are designed to withstand 450 gals. After reevaluating their proximity to a Tokai earthquake's epicenter, Reactors Nos. 3 and 4 were designed to withstand 600 gals. The earthquake that struck southern Hyogo Prefecture was recorded to have 820 gals, but if it were to occur over solid foundations, the force would be reduced by one-half or one-third. As a comparison, in the western United States, a region that is frequented by earthquakes, permission to construct a nuclear power plant is granted if the plant is able to withstand 500 gals.

In 2005 Reactors Nos. 1–5 at the Hamaoka Nuclear Power Plant underwent large-scale reinforcement. The construction was to focus on reinforcing the steel frames of the plant's exhaust pipes, adding support equipment for pipelines, and increasing its earthquake resistance to 1,000 gals.

The task for the future is an early investigation and assessment of the degree of earthquake resistance of nuclear power plants that have become old or weakened over time. Furthermore, the establishment of safety for all nuclear reactor cores and turbine structures, the reevaluation of active fault lines, and the reexamination of manuals for operators of nuclear facilities during an earthquake are necessary.

In any case nuclear power plants that are built nowadays are based on the "Earthquake Resistant Design Examination Guidelines Regarding Nuclear Power Reactor Facilities," which is at the time of this writing more than twenty-five years old. During that time we have learned much more about earthquakes, and improvements have been made to the construction of nuclear reactors. It is essential to reevaluate the current situation.

As we have seen from the Chernobyl disaster in the past and the Fukushima disaster more recently, once a nuclear disaster occurs, it will travel beyond a nation's borders and affect a large region and perhaps many countries. Therefore nuclear disasters especially need to be prevented.

CHAPTER 4

Tsunamis

The Horror of Tsunamis

The crest of the wave pushes along followed by a giant wave. Without any means of escaping, people are swallowed up by the giant wave. The ferocious energy of the ocean engulfs the beachside pool. Mass amounts of murky water invade the city as the water swallows up everything in its path from cars to houses to people. Countless muddy corpses lay on the streets. No matter how many times one sees the images, people are awestruck and fear the violent energy.

More than 220,000 people lost their lives or went missing in the tsunami caused by the 2004 Indian Ocean Earthquake. At first it was broadcast that the deaths were in the thousands, but as days passed, the numbers increased dramatically.

There were so many deaths and missing persons from this tragedy because of the general ignorance about tsunamis. People went out toward the sea to catch the stranded fish when the tide pulled out, not knowing that it was a sign that a tsunami was coming, and after the first wave of the tsunami some even went back out toward the beach to see what had happened. Generally it is said that if you climb to the second story of a concrete building with reinforced steel, you will be safe from a tsunami. Most people did not run for higher ground but instead ran parallel to the tsunami. On land the tsunami is said to have traveled at 36 kilometers per hour. It is not possible to escape a tsunami traveling at that speed on foot. Furthermore, nobody expected a giant tsunami to surge toward Sri Lanka, which is located 1,600 kilometers away from the epicenter of the earthquake.

The Pacific Tsunami Warning Center (PTWC) in Hawaii was established after many of the Pacific island nations had been heavily damaged by the tsunami following the Great Chilean Earthquake of 1960.[1] The center has observation machines one kilometer offshore various Pacific island nations that monitor wave heights, and it shares the information regionally. In 1996 the center also set up sensors on the seabed that observe wave heights and transmit the data to a satellite. The 2004 tsunami that struck Sumatra was detected by the PTWC, but there was no system in place then to relay the information.

Tsunamis occur where there are earthquakes. Many tsunamis have struck Japan in the past:

1896   Meiji Sanriku Tsunami: over 20,000 deaths

1933   Sanriku Tsunami: death toll, including missing persons: 3,064

1944   Tonankai Earthquake: death toll, including missing persons: 1,233, with 17,599 homes destroyed

1946   Showa Nankai Earthquake: At around 4:30 a.m., December 21, the tide rapidly withdrew from the coast of Tanabe City, Wakayama Prefecture. Soon after a tsunami pushed toward land with a loud roar. Within ten minutes all 10 km of the city's coastline were struck by waves 4–5 meters high and waves as high as six meters pushed into the city. Wakayama Prefecture suffered a death/missing persons toll of 269 from this tsunami. The earthquake itself killed 1,330 people, destroyed 11,591 houses, and flooded another 1,451.

1960   Tsunami caused by the Great Chilean Earthquake resulted in the deaths of 142 people across Japan.

1993   Earthquake offshore of Hokkaido's southwest. Three minutes later a tsunami hit the west coast of Okujiri Island. The tsunami left Okujiri Island in rubble and the charred frames of houses. It is estimated that the tsunami's height was fifteen meters when it hit the coast and that it was able to travel to areas 30.6 meters above sea level. This tsunami killed 220 people.

Japan is an island nation surrounded by water and is frequented by earthquakes. It is understandable that tsunamis hit Japan, and indeed it would not make any sense were it otherwise. The Meteorological Agency attempts to issue a tsunami warning within three minutes after an earthquake is detected based on simulations of earthquake and tsunami patterns. The agency's has about one hundred thousand simulation patterns. When an earthquake's scale and location are inputted, the agency determines the possibilities of a tsunami. This same information is televised.

Should a Tokai earthquake occur, it was estimated that the worst-case death toll from the tsunami will be over 2,200 in an area that extends from Chiba Prefecture to Wakayama Prefecture. This number was substantially revised in 2012 to at least 323,000.[2] The death toll will reach the estimated numbers only if the residents lack information and if the floodgates fail to operate.

If both Tonankai and Nankai earthquakes strike, the death toll from the subsequent tsunami is expected to be about 8,600 (from Aichi Prefecture to Kochi Prefecture), a number that has also been updated into the many tens of thousands. If all three earthquakes strike—Tokai, Tonankai, and Nankai—the death toll from the subsequent tsunami was expected to be over 18,000 but is now in the hundreds of thousands.

Shizuoka Prefecture is expected to receive the heaviest damage from a Tokai earthquake; Suruga Bay is expected to be hit by a tsunami at least ten meters high within five minutes, and Enshunan is expected to be hit by a tsunami at least as high as seven meters. Earlier estimates suggested approximately 37.9 square kilometers of coastline facing the Pacific Ocean are expected to be under water after these respective tsunami waves.

The expected structural damage from the tsunami was, prior to March 11, as follows: 2,200 buildings completely destroyed; 11,000 buildings partially destroyed; 15,000 buildings with flood damage. Just within Shizuoka Prefecture alone, the death toll due to the tsunami as of 2006 was expected to be 220, and 900 people would suffer serious injuries. Now the figures are much higher, in the many thousands. In the current estimate Shizuoka would experience 109,000 deaths from a megaquake and tsunami.[3]

What if an earthquake hits during the summer? Summer is the peak season for beachgoers, attracting over ten thousand people on a single day. A tsunami is expected to arrive within five to ten minutes after the initial earthquake. Many people on the beach will not be able to escape, making it almost impossible to estimate the loss of life at the beach.

Consider this possible scenario: A tsunami arrives several minutes after an initial quake in the western and urban districts of Tosa Shimizu City in southwestern Kochi Prefecture. Six thousand people (one-third of the population of the city) live in those districts and are expected to be submerged under water after an eight-meter-high tsunami hits the region, according to pre-March 11 estimates (thirty-four meters in the higher end of the current estimates). The whole city, including all of its important infrastructure, will be destroyed, with the possible exception of the city hall and an elementary school, which are located on a hill twelve meters above sea level.

This is the result of a tsunami damage assessment conducted by Kochi Prefecture regarding Tosa Shimizu City. The prefecture has five different scenarios basing the epicenter of the earthquake in the Nankai Trough. Tosa Shimizu City, which is located in southern Shikoku Island, will be the worst affected by such a tsunami. According to the simulation, the tsunami will not hit only Tosa Shimizu; within thirty minutes of the earthquake all of Kochi Prefecture's coast will be hit by tsunami waves.

In the case that Tonankai and Nankai earthquakes occur simultaneously, computer simulations based on hazard maps have calculated the estimated damage from a subsequent tsunami. The simulations also estimate the death toll based on several patterns or situations. One scenario takes into account the time it will take for residents to evacuate the area after disaster information has been broadcast by the media or local government through loudspeakers or mobile loudspeakers. In the simulation, when an evacuation took place immediately after a warning was issued, there were no deaths. However, if the evacuation is delayed by twenty minutes after the earthquake hits, it was previously s predicted that the tsunami would claim 2,700 lives. These predictions reflect the situation of the 2004 Sumatra earthquake tsunami but have further been revised. In Sumatra the tsunami swallowed up people while other people stood a couple of meters away recording the whole thing with a video camera. A height difference of one meter is sometimes the division between life and death.

The height of a tsunami is determined by the height of the wave at the time it reaches land. A ten-meter tsunami is not a ten-meter wave but an increase in the sea level by ten meters. Topography further affects the destruction as tsunami waves get concentrated in narrow bays, inlets, or rivers.

The following statements are from eyewitnesses of tsunamis as reported on the many television broadcasts afterward.

> "I saw the tsunami approach the land from a distance. It was as if the sea pulled out, then the water gradually engulfed the land."
> "Just when the water disappeared from the coast, the sea level began to rise as it headed toward land."
> "Just as I thought the tide had left, the next second a giant wall of water was approaching toward land."
> "The water pulled out fast, and within a few minutes it seemed like the whole ocean's sea level had increased."

"Tsunami" refers to a giant mass of seawater movement, and it can be divided into two types. The first, referred to as a "drawback tsunami," is caused by the springing movement of earthquake faults; the second is a tsunami caused by an increase of sea level. The tsunamis of the Indian Ocean in 2004 began with a drawback tsunami that went east toward Thailand while an increasing-sea-level tsunami headed west toward India. The tsunami in Sumatra, as we saw from the images, resembled a giant wave that swallowed everything in its path, flooding an entire city.

Wooden buildings will be partially destroyed by a one-meter tsunami but will be completely destroyed by a two-meter tsunami. Steel-reinforced concrete buildings have been tested to withstand tsunamis up to five meters high, but there are no data recorded beyond this test. During the Indian Ocean tsunami a 6.3-meter wave struck the island of Phuket, located in southern Thailand, and destroyed the walls of a steel-reinforced concrete building, leaving only the pillars standing.

Anticipating such situations, the Japanese Ministry of Land,

Infrastructure, and Transport began drafting a new construction standard for houses and buildings to increase their resistance to tsunamis.

In 1854 the Ansei Tokai Earthquake and Ansei Nankai Earthquake occurred at the same time, sending seven-meter-high tsunamis toward Shimoda and ten-meter-high tsunamis to Ise, Kumano, and Tosa. Records from that day show that the tsunamis destroyed all bridges, and boats were carried onto land by the tsunamis. If both a Tonankai and Nankai earthquake occur at the same time, it is expected that within ten minutes tsunamis with an average height of five meters and perhaps as high as twelve meters will arrive. If floodgates are damaged by the earthquakes, their failure to close will cause massive amounts of water from the tsunamis to flood the cities. There is also the chance that large container ships, oil tankers, and cargo ships that were not able to escape to deeper seas will be carried onto shore or into the cities, causing great damage. Oil leaks from the damaged ships will also cause pollution in those waters, which are very likely to be washed into the cities, increasing the hazards to the destroyed cities.[4]

In June 2005 the experts' committee of the Central Disaster Management Council published its quake magnitude estimates for six locations of trench-type earthquakes near Hokkaido and northeast Japan. The committee also estimated the tsunami heights for Tokatsu and offshore Nemuro if the "Earthquake Every 500 Years" (a theory formally introduced in the committee's working group) and the "Meiji Sanriku Earthquake" (of June 1896) scenarios were to happen again. The Tokatsu-Nemuro region is the meeting point for two plates—the North American Plate moves underneath the Pacific Plate, and historically the region has been known as an area frequented by earthquakes.

Earthquake off coast of Etorofu Island	Magnitude 8.4; seismic intensity level 6
Earthquake off coast of Shikotan Island	Magnitude 8.3; seismic intensity level 6
Earthquake off coast of Nemuro	Magnitude 8.3; seismic intensity level 6

Earthquake off coast of Tokatsu	Magnitude 8.2; seismic intensity level 6
"Earthquake Every 500 Years"	Magnitude 8.6 with 15-meter-plus tsunami
Earthquake off coast of north Sanriku	Magnitude 8.3–8.4; seismic intensity level 6
Earthquake off coast of Miyagi Prefecture	Magnitude 7.6–8.2; seismic intensity level 6
Meiji Sanriku Earthquake	Magnitude 8.6 with 20-meter-plus tsunami

Source: Central Disaster Management Council Report, 2005.

"Honestly, there is no way to prevent them. All we can do is warn everyone to quickly evacuate to high ground," the deputy director of planning and commerce of Hitaka City, Hokkaido Prefecture, admitted.

Disaster Prevention and Its Defects in the Tokai Region

Seven hundred and twenty km/h is not the speed of an airplane but that of a tsunami. A tsunami's speed varies with the depth of the ocean. At a depth of four thousand meters a tsunami travels at 712 km/h, and when it reaches a depth of two hundred meters over the continental shelf, its speed is reduced to 160 km/h. It is much faster than the speed of local trains that run in the country. When a tsunami reaches land, it will travel at a speed of 30 km/h. It will be impossible to escape it on foot. People will get swallowed up by it. In other words, humans will not be able to escape a tsunami by running on level ground. People that have already escaped to higher ground will be the only survivors.

A tsunami is an enormous body of water backed by the ocean moving toward land. It increases its speed and height when the geography allows it to concentrate its mass of water. A tsunami can concentrate its mass, particularly inside of bays and especially in bays shaped in a "V." The speed of a tsunami also changes based on the depth of the ocean, and thus it is not only the shape of the bottom of the sea but also its depth that can cause a tsunami to concentrate in certain areas.

Damage from a Tokai earthquake and tsunami will be concentrated in Shizuoka Prefecture. Within five minutes of the quake, tsunamis as high as ten meters will be expected in the coastal areas of Suruga. Seven-meter tsunamis will arrive within ten minutes near Enshunan, and within thirty minutes a tsunami of the same caliber will be expected near the coastal region of the Izu Peninsula.

The importance of tsunami hazard maps has been stressed above to prepare residents and visitors for tsunamis. These maps should contain information on regions that are expected to be affected by a tsunami and the expected level of flooding. The maps would be meaningless if they did not contain information on evacuation routes and evacuation sites.

In May 2004 the Ministry of Land, Infrastructure, and Transport compiled a study on the official production and publication of Tsunami hazard maps and reports on the quake resistance of sea walls along the coast. The study showed that of the 991 cities and towns listed as danger zones in the event of a tsunami, only 95 of them (9.6 percent) had produced Tsunami hazard maps, while 896 cities and towns (90.4 percent) had none. Even those that had published such maps failed to list evacuation sites. Furthermore, 60 percent of the cities and towns had not conducted quake resistance research on their sea walls, and most of them were also behind or lacking in this field.

Iwate Prefecture was the only exception; it was the only one to have a 100 percent completion rate. Iwate must have a high awareness about tsunamis given the fact that it has suffered numerous tsunamis in the past. Some maps even show the expected damage in a time progression from a tsunami caused by an earthquake off the coast of Miyagi Prefecture. Iwate Prefecture spent 200 million yen ($2 million) to create these maps. As noted at the time, there was a 99 percent possibility for the occurrence of an earthquake off the coast of Miyagi (magnitude 7.6–8.2) over the next thirty years.[5]

According to research conducted by the Cabinet Office, 56 percent of medical facilities met the requirements for earthquake resistant construction, while only 46 percent of elementary and middle schools, which are used as evacuation sites, met the requirements nationwide. This study shows that disaster prevention awareness varies from region to region in Japan.

However, it is difficult to tell each city and town to create its own hazard maps since an extensive knowledge of tsunamis is required in order to perfect the maps. The management of statistics, computer programs, money, and manpower is also required to create effective and reliable hazard maps. In order to create quality maps, the government should take the initiative to set standards, train experts in the field, and deploy experts across the nation. It goes without saying that the cooperation of the experts and local residents is necessary. While it should not be rushed haphazardly, it is a priority that needs to be addressed as soon as possible.

A tsunami warning was issued after two earthquakes occurred off the coast of the Kii Peninsula on September 5, 2004. According to the Ministry of Internal Affairs and Communications' Fire and Disaster Management Agency (Sōmushō Shōbōchō), of forty-two cities, towns, and villages that required evacuation advisories in Aichi, Mie, and Wakayama Prefectures, only twelve local administrations issued warnings. These twelve had established proper evacuation routes and evacuation sites. In other words, a high awareness of disasters is a crucial element in disaster prevention and in saving lives.

Two types of tsunami evacuation warnings are announced to local residents by cities, towns, and villages, as regulated under the Disaster Measures Basic Law: an Evacuation Advisory (Hinan Kankoku) and a Mandatory Evacuation Order (Hinan Shiji). The Mandatory Evacuation Order is announced only at times of serious emergency.

There have been cases of city officials going to the coastline to confirm if a tsunami were coming, only to put off issuing a warning or to refrain from issuing a warning. The rules of thumb for tsunamis are to never go near the coast after an earthquake. What really is needed now is for officials to be properly educated about tsunamis.

What about the residents? A study conducted by Gunma University (Gunma Daigaku) looked at the level of residents' awareness of tsunamis in Owase City, Mie Prefecture.[6] When an earthquake shook Owase City at 7:07 p.m. on September 5, 2004, 81.7 percent of its residents said they thought of the possibility of a tsunami. When a second earthquake followed at 11:57 p.m., 81 percent of the residents worried about a tsunami. However, when the first earthquake hit, only 10.3 percent actually evacuated. When the second earthquake hit, 22.3 percent evacuated to designated sites. The second earthquake had a higher evacuation rate possibly due to the "what-if" factor from the first earthquake. But when a third earthquake hit, attitudes shifted slightly. Far fewer people evacuated, and the most common response was, "[We] decided not to evacuate after talking it over with our neighbors." Further, after the first earthquake, 20.1 percent went to the coast to look at the tide, and after the second, 15.3 percent went to the coast.

Studies by the Central Disaster Management Council found that within ten minutes after a Tonankai or Nankai earthquake has struck, a tsunami of at least five meters or more will be expected to hit Mie Prefecture. The 1944 Tonankai Earthquake was followed by a nine-meter tsunami that claimed the lives of 1,223 people.

Professor Katada Toshiaki of Gunma University's School of Technology (Kōgakubu) created a simulation that takes into account residents' conscious evacuations from tsunamis. Katada's simulation calculated that the next Tonankai earthquake death toll would reach at least 2,800. Katada says, "It is expected that in the next Tonankai/Nankai earthquake, a tsunami of at least six meters will hit Owase City within twenty minutes. There will be no time for the residents to waste. Proper evacuation training, based on the simulation and the habit of immediate evacuation after an earthquake, is the only way to prevent a high death toll." According to the simulation, there will be no deaths caused by the tsunami if immediate evacuation takes place after the earthquake. However, if people wait three minutes after evacuation orders are announced, 305 people will likely lose their lives. The golden rule to surviving an imminent tsunami is to get away from the coast after an earthquake as soon as possible and evacuate to higher ground immediately.

Isolation of the Tokai Region: Tokai Shinkansen
Railway and Tohoku Expressway

"We cannot hope for aid to arrive immediately," an official from Yokosuka City, Kanagawa Prefecture, acknowledged.[7] Yokosuka is located at the tip of the Miura Peninsula. Landslides caused by earthquakes can easily block roadways to and from the city, isolating it from outside aid. Yokosuka City has an inventory of blankets, emergency toilets, and food such as biscuits and rice (enough for four hundred thousand people), stocked in empty elementary classrooms labeled "disaster prevention storage warehouses" (bōsai sōko). At the time of this writing, there are twenty-three such warehouse sites located throughout the city. There are forty-five emergency water tanks at elementary schools and parks that are designated as evacuation sites. These tanks can supply twenty liters of water for thirty days to every resident of the city.

People traveling to Kobe City during the Great Hanshin-Awaji Earthquake must have been surprised by the traffic jams on every road leading into the city. Even six months after the disaster, functional roads were very limited, causing massive traffic jams. Such traffic jams made it difficult to travel by car and also affected the efficiency of emergency vehicles. Normally, even on busy days, it takes at most one hour from Osaka to Kobe on the expressway, but during the disaster it took twelve hours to transport medical supplies.

The collapsed expressway and destroyed buildings were cleared in a timely manner, but the main roads remained congested with people and vehicles. Many people expressed concern that the expressway rubble was removed without a proper researching of why the expressway had collapsed.

When the 2004 Niigata-Chuetsu Earthquake struck Niigata Prefecture, it left the Joetsu Shinkansen trains derailed, and traffic was stopped from the Muika Machi Interchange on the Kanetsu Expressway (Kanetsu Jidōshadō) to Nagaoka Junction due to damage from the earthquake. There were problems with the delivery of rescue relief supplies and the transportation of the injured to medical facilities because the main transportation route from Tokyo to Niigata had been paralyzed, but surprisingly the rescue went smoothly. Major transportation issues between Tokyo and Niigata were avoided due to the fact that there were two alternative routes: the Banetsudo Expressway from the east and the Joshinetsudo Expressway from the west. Vehicles transporting rescue relief goods were allowed to use the expressways free of charge, and a chaotic situation was avoided.

But what if a similar earthquake hit Tokyo? If an inland earthquake were to hit the capital, Tokyo Metro Route 7 and National Road Route 246, which connects the inner regions to Tamagawa, would both be shut down. In other words, it would be extremely difficult to enter or leave central Tokyo. Also all subways and railways would stop; if the earthquake were to hit at noon, 3.9 million Tokyo metropolitan residents would be stranded and unable to return home, while an additional 6.5 million commuters from the three surrounding prefectures of Chiba, Saitama, and Kanagawa would be also stranded.[8] Vehicles on the roads cleared for emergency services on the highways would also have a difficult time moving due to collapsed buildings and submerged roads. The damage can be expected to increase as fire trucks, police cars, and other emergency vehicles are unable to respond due to damage and debris on the roadways. It is a matter of urgency to fully connect the metropolitan expressways and roadways.

The estimated affected disaster area of a Tokai, Nankai, and Tonankai earthquake spans one thousand kilometers, from the Izu Peninsula to Cape Ashizuri in Shikoku, and regions on the Pacific Belt zone from Tokyo to Osaka will suffer damage from such an earthquake and tsunami. The following were the expected heights of the tsunami for each prefecture or area prior to the March 11 disaster:

Shizuoka Prefecture	3 meters
Aichi Prefecture, outer sea	2 meters
Ise/Mikawa Bay	1 meter
Southern Mie Prefecture	4 meters
Wakayama Prefecture	10 meters-plus
Osaka Prefecture	1 meter
Hyogo Prefecture (Inland Sea)	1 meter

Southern Awaji Island	4 meters
Tokushima Prefecture	6 meters
Kochi Prefecture	8 meters
Ehime Prefecture (Uwa coast)	2 meters

Source: Central Disaster Management Council Report, 2005. Note: These figures were substantially and in some cases exponentially increased in 2012.

Six hundred kilometers separate Tokyo and Osaka, with Nagoya in the middle. These cities are connected by the Tokaido Shinkansen line, Tomei Expressway, Meishin Expressway, Narita Airport, Tokyo International Airport (Haneda), Nagoya Airport, Osaka International Airport (Itami), Kobe Airport, Chubu International Airport, and Kansai International Airport. What if the Tokaido Shinkansen, the Tomei Expressway, and the Meishin Expressway were blocked or otherwise unusable? Nagoya Airport, Osaka Airport, and Kobe Airport could probably not quickly be utilized either, as it would be necessary to check the condition of the runways and possibly repair them. Kansai International Airport, Chubu International Airport, and Kobe Airport may possibly be impacted by a tsunami since they are built on landfill out in the respective bays.[9] If such blockages or tsunami damage were to happen, cities, towns, and villages in the regions of the Pacific Belt zone, including Nagoya, would become isolated landlocked islands in and of themselves. For example, the Chuo Expressway is used by drivers to go from Tokyo to Nagoya, while the Meishin Expressway is used to get to Nagoya from Osaka. However, if Osaka is damaged, the Chuo Expressway is the only option.

In 1979 there was a large-scale fire in the Nihonzaka Tunnel between the Shizuoka Interchange and the Yaizu Interchange on the Tomei Expressway. It took a week for the tunnel to be reopened, and that was for just one lane. Similar accidents could occur in all the various tunnels along the Pacific coast highways from Tokyo to Shikoku. Roads along mountains are most likely to be affected by landslides as well. Mie Prefecture and Wakayama Prefecture face a strong likelihood of becoming isolated if roads along the Pacific coast on the Izu Peninsula become buried by landslides or destroyed in a tsunami.[10] When one considers such possibilities, one cannot complain about the construction of "useless" expressways. In fact it may be necessary to build roads, no matter how small scale, in order to help in the recovery and reconstruction during and after disasters.

U.S. forces in Japan offered to use their equipment, including their aircraft carrier and amphibious ships, as hospital ships immediately after the Great Hanshin-Awaji Earthquake. The aircraft carrier *Kitty Hawk*, stationed in Yokosuka, could have been used along with other ships, such as those from the 31st Marine Expeditionary Unit stationed in Okinawa (with ships docked in Sasebo, Nagasaki Prefecture, for refitting and repairs), for the treatment of the injured and as an evacuation shelter while anchored offshore Kobe. The Japanese government turned down the U.S. offer. There were probably voices of opposition to American forces leaving their bases in Japan, even to provide disaster relief, to conduct military operations within Japan.

The Self-Defense Forces deployed about 680 vessels during the Great Hanshin-Awaji Earthquake. The ships were used to transport disaster relief aid/goods, supply water and food, and set up baths for victims of the disaster, in addition to setting up tents for the GSDF on disaster relief missions. It is disappointing to learn that none of the vessels was used for medical assistance. There are examples of volunteer ships leaving Rokko Island, where the Kobe City Medical Center General Hospital (Kōbe Shiritsu Iryō Sentaa Chūō Shimin Byōin) is located, to transport dialysis patients. Ships that were equipped with intensive care units, dialysis facilities, and helipads would have been extremely useful to have then.

While the Japanese government considered that an American aircraft carrier was unnecessary at the time of the Kobe disaster, such will probably not be true if Tokai, Tonankai, and Nankai earthquakes simultaneously hit Japan. There are no means of transporting one hundred thousand injured people if the roads and railways are cut off along the Pacific coast from Tokyo to the Shikoku region. It is expected that within a week there would be 4.44 million refugees (or internally displaced persons), and it would be extremely difficult to send relief supplies to them.

Izu is the name of the disaster response patrol ship of the Fifth District Coast Guard. *Izu*, 110 meters in length and 3,700 tons, is equipped with a medical section in which emergency surgery can be performed, living quarters for 120 people, and seawater distilling equipment with a storage capacity of 800 tons. *Izu* was designed and created after the lessons learned from the Great Hanshin-Awaji disaster and was deployed for the 2004 Niigata-Chuetsu Earthquake relief mission.

Japan needs to start considering such realistic issues as using the Self-Defense Forces' vessels or constructing hospital ships. If there is a strong opposition toward the SDF's acquiring hospital ships, the Ministry of Health, Labor, and Welfare should build these ships for the use of the SDF, as was done in the case of the Antarctica research vessel built by the former Ministry of Education to be used by the Maritime Self-Defense Force. There is an immediate need for Japan to consider large-scale relief efforts conducted from the sea.[11]

Underground Malls of Osaka and Nagoya

"I pray that a caring person will put ink into the engravings to make them more legible as time goes on," says the last sentence of the epigraph on a stone monument erected near the Taisho Bridge (Taishōbashi) in Naniwa, Osaka. "Records of the Great Earthquake and Ryogawaguchi Tsunami" is the title engraved into the stone monument. The epigraph is quite long, but this is how it goes:

> On June 14, 1854, seventh year of Kaei, there was a great earthquake that shook around noon. The frightened citizens of Osaka stood near the river as four to five days passed, and they lived in fear of an aftershock. There were many deaths in Mie and Nara from this earthquake.
>
> The same year, at 8 a.m. on November 14, another great earthquake hit. The people, wary from the previous earthquake, had built sheds on open land, where children and the elderly evacuated. Some evacuated on boats, thinking that it would be safer to be on the river during an earthquake. Another great earthquake hit the next day around 4 p.m. Houses collapsed and fires broke out.

Just when the chaos seemed to settle in the evening, a tsunami violently surged in with a loud, thundering sound.

A wave the size of a mountain swept through the Ajigawa River to the mouth of the Kizugawa River. Higashibori was submerged under 1.4 meters of muddy water. The anchors and hawsers of boats, large and small, docked along the Ryogawa River, were ripped apart. The Ajigawa Bridge, Kamei Bridge, Taka Bridge, Mizuwake Bridge, Kurogane Bridge, Hiyoshi Bridge, Shiomi Bridge, Saiwai Bridge, Sumiyoshi Bridge, and Kaneya Bridge were all destroyed by the intense backflow of the river. Panic and confusion caused by the overflow of water onto the roads led to many people getting swept up into the river and drowning.

A large ship was turned on its side by the backflow, blocking the water flow of the Dotonbori River, where the Oguro Bridge is. Other ships coming from the river mouth struck the overturned ship, washing up on top of the bridge. Debris and the wreckage of boats filled the rivers running south to north, the Dotonbori River to Matsugahana's Kizu River, west of Oguro Bridge, destroying small buildings along the river. The noise of debris crashing into the city and people yelling for help filled the entire area. The violent backwater carrying debris made it impossible to rescue the stranded residents and many died. People who feared that the tsunami would surge onto the docks of Shima-no-Uchi rushed to evacuate to Uemachi City.

There were also stories about many people drowning as they fled the tsunami on small boats when an earthquake struck on October 4, 1707 (fourth year of Hoei). As time passed, those that could retell the stories were long gone, so many people fell victim the same way again.

These disasters are sure to happen as well in the future, so when an earthquake strikes, it is important to be aware of a possible tsunami and never try to escape by boat. Also, buildings will collapse and fires are likely to break out. It is essential to keep important documents and money safe, but more important, it is crucial to keep the possibility of fires in mind. Boats that are docked along rivers should be brought to higher ground away from the reach of the tsunami.

Tsunamis do not necessary always come from the ocean. Some emerge from the ocean floor, and fields near the ocean can have muddy water flowing out from the ground. In this earthquake, such a phenomenon was seen at the lake in Furuichi, Habikino City. Water overflowed from the lake and went on to wash away many houses. People living near the coast, large rivers, and lakes need to be aware of this kind of tsunami.

The people that experienced this tsunami know now, but it is important to understand that the force of a tsunami is not the same as a storm surge. Pray for the souls of the victims. This is a poorly written message, but it will be recorded here. I pray that a caring person will put ink into the engravings to make them more legible as time goes on, and let this story be told (again and again).

Built in July 1855 (second year of Ansei).

More than 150 years ago, after an earthquake far offshore of the Kii Peninsula shook Osaka, a tsunami hit the city of Osaka. This was the Ansei Nankai Earthquake. The monument described above records the experiences of a man who survived that earthquake and tsunami in the Edo period. His experiences can be related to the modern day and should serve as an example to us—a so-called lesson learned.

Kyoto University's Disaster Prevention Research Institute Center for Mega Disaster Research (Kyōto Daigaku Bōsai Kenkyūsho Kyodai Saigai Kenkyū Sentaa), led by Dr. Kawata Yoshiaki, conducted a tsunami simulation for a Nankai earthquake scenario. The simulation predicted the following: "Nankai earthquake hits. The tsunami destroys embankments on the coast. The tsunami will travel upstream along rivers from Osaka Bay. It will flow into central Osaka from Nakanoshima Island, about eight kilometers upstream. Within two hours 50,000 square meters of water will flood the underground malls."

In the 1854 Ansei Nankai Earthquake, there were at least eight hundred victims in Osaka alone. If both a Tokai and Nankai earthquake strike at the same time, Osaka will have a 5-plus seismic intensity. What is even more worrisome is the subsequent tsunami. The tsunami, originating in the Pacific Ocean, will pass through the Kii Channel, enter the Kitan Strait bouncing off of Awaji Island, and push its way through Osaka like it did 150 years ago.

The first tsunami will arrive within two hours of the earthquake, with a height of 2.1 meters, and the second tsunami, of about 2.5 meters, will arrive fifty minutes after it. Both tsunamis will be traveling at a speed of about 36 km/h.

The tsunamis will flood into the inland areas, traveling upstream along rivers. The only difference between the 1854 situation and now is that Osaka has not only grown above ground but underground as well, with subways, walkways, stores, and restaurants—a city below the city. Further, the foundation underneath this city is sinking due to the pumping out of underground water. Osaka's Umeda underground mall is the most complicated of its kind in Japan, and tens of thousands of people go there daily. The tsunami will flood this underground city.

Floodgates have been built to counter the threat from flooding and tsunamis. The tsunami will make its way upstream along the Ajigawa, Kizugawa, and Shirinashigawa Rivers from Osaka Bay. The city is protected by about nine hundred embankments, but these embankments were designed to counter storm surges, not tsunamis. Moreover, research shows that it takes almost six hours to close all of the floodgates. There is a possibility that the tsunami will easily flow into the Central Ward (Chuo-ku) of Osaka.

Three-meter high embankments run along 160 kilometers of Osaka's waterline. According to officials in the Public Works Department of Osaka Prefecture (Ōsakafu Dobokubu), tsunamis would be lower than the height of the embankments and thus, according to them, the embankments would protect the city from the tsunami.

Reinforced floodgates have been built along the Yodogawa, Yamatogawa, and Ishizugawa Rivers. To prevent floods, gates have been built in the entrances of the seven thousand embankments also. However, as seen in the following list, there are many areas of concern with the current situation:

The embankment gates will not close. It takes five minutes and four people to completely shut each gate. There are seven hundred gates in total that absolutely have to be closed, and it is impossible to close all the gates within two hours.

Possibilities of tsunamis higher than the embankments. A tsunami is a large mass of seawater. If objects obstruct its path, the tsunami will increase in height. In other words, if the tidal wave hits the embankment, the mass of the tsunami will increase and eventually flow over it.

The destruction of embankments and floodgates caused by seismic intensity 5-plus earthquake. During the Great Hanshin-Awaji Earthquake, many of the embankments were destroyed from the earthquake and the liquefaction effect.

Ships colliding and destroying embankments and floodgates. There are well over a hundred ships docked at Osaka Port daily. Unlike large waves caused by typhoons, a tsunami is an enormous movement of the ocean. If ships are not able to escape to deeper seas, the strong current from the tsunami will take the ships with it. If a ship that weighs over ten thousand tons collides into the embankment at a speed of 50 km/h, it will destroy the embankment. A two- to three-meter-high tsunami will then flow over the damaged embankment and make its way inland. If this ship happens to be an oil tanker, oil will spill and flow into the city. After the tsunami struck Sumatra in 2004, a fifty-meter-long ship was washed up onshore three kilometers from the nearest coast.

Timber washed away from lumber yards destroying floodgates and bridges. There are photographs of timber dispersed all over the place after the tsunami hit Sumatra.

Osaka City's Taisho Ward (Taishō-ku), where the aforementioned monument is located, sits at sea level. Simulations show that if the floodgates do not close or embankments are destroyed, a tsunami of two meters will flood through the city. The tsunami will then head toward the Umeda and Nanba areas at a speed of 30 km/h as it engulfs areas that sit at or below sea level. In Umeda there is a large underground arcade, called Whitey Umeda, where more than sixty thousand people shop daily. If all eighty-eight entrances to Whitey Umeda cannot be shut and if the tsunami is higher than the water blockade boards that are placed at the tops of stairwells, water from the tsunami will flow into the arcade. Until a couple of years ago a water blockade board weighed twenty kilograms and took four people to carry it. The old boards have been replaced with new ones that can be set up in five minutes by one person. However, Umeda sits one meter above sea level. If a two-meter tsunami comes, the water blockade boards will be useless.

Many people have witnessed roads getting flooded as the lids of manholes burst near the coast during a typhoon. Such bursting is caused by high waves moving upstream through the sewage pipes. The same will happen during a tsunami.

In 2004 many rivers flooded across Japan due to typhoons, heavy rainfall, and storm surges. The floods submerged the metropolis roads in Shinjuku, causing damage in shopping districts and underground malls. The time has certainly come for cities that have underground arcades to devise effective measures against storms, floods, and tsunamis.

After anticipating such situations, Osaka Prefecture decided to establish a "tsunami station" by 2008. The tsunami station will broadcast evacuation orders during a tsunami and remotely control the opening and shutting of the floodgates. It will also prepare an exhibit aimed at educating the public on the importance of understanding tsunamis and evacuation procedures. The tsunami station will manage the "Tsunami Disaster Prevention Information System." Speakers are to be established near embankments, factories by the coast, wharves, and yacht harbors that will alert the public to the arrival of a tsunami. It will also establish a "Command of Security and Orders during Disaster Times System," which will send state-of-emergency messages to the cell phones of police officers and city officials.

The typhoons that hit Japan from the spring to the fall of 2004 brought storm surges, floods, and strong winds along with them, causing much damage. Seawater carried by strong winds accumulated onto power lines and transformers and caused many power outages in many areas. Many can recall the headlights of automobiles suddenly turning on and horns going off with them. Further, cars that were exposed to seawater would run normally but suddenly stop working. The adhesion of sea water causes the electrical wires in a car to short-circuit, damaging the wiring system.

Even after the seawater recedes after a tsunami, a flooded city will need to replace most or all of its electrical equipment. Moreover, the reliability and durability of the underground water pipes and gas pipes cannot be guaranteed. Damage from salt water needs to be considered when taking measures against tsunamis.

At the Cabinet Office's Central Disaster Management Council, the government has hypothesized the damage Japan would suffer from an earthquake expected to occur in the near future. The citizens of Japan need to fully understand and prepare for the threat that is coming.

According to the *Sankei Shimbun*, one of the main newspapers in Japan and the most conservative,

> The Cabinet Office has decided to reevaluate the tsunami damage assessment it published in 2003, which estimated a death toll of twelve thousand people. Limited awareness of the danger of tsunamis caused many deaths in the 2004 Sumatra tsunami. Taking that into account, there is a high possibility that the new estimated death toll will be greater. Local governments estimate that the death toll could be far greater than the 2003 estimate. Some experts estimate that the death toll will be around ten thousand people. There is a great need to reevaluate and reinforce the new tsunami measures.[12]

How can we evaluate a policy that changes with every little variation in the estimates?

CHAPTER 5

Disaster Prevention and Reduction

Headquarters for Disaster Measures

On both sides of the main highway there are well-constructed buildings and a vast piece of land one kilometer north off of Tachikawa Station on the Chuo Line of Japan Railways. This is the Tachikawa Disaster Base.

According to an official from the Disaster Response Headquarters Reserve Facility (Saigai Taisaku Honbu Yobi Shisetsu) of the Cabinet Office's Disaster Prevention Division,

> The south Kanto region has been frequented by many large trench-type earthquakes, in the magnitude 8 class, that have an epicenter at Sagami Trough, similar to the Great Kanto Earthquake that occurred on September 1, 1923. In between the large trench-type earthquakes there have been several local earthquakes of magnitude 7 class, and it has been pointed out that another local earthquake is imminent. Large earthquakes that strike right below major cities will cause great damage, as we have seen in the January 1995 Great Hanshin-Awaji Earthquake. From the Great Hanshin-Awaji disaster, we have learned that it is necessary for air transportation to bring aid and relief supplies to the disaster sites. The Tachikawa Disaster Base is a facility that has been jointly managed by the national government, the Tokyo Metropolitan Government, and various organizations in preparation for

a large-scale disaster in the south Kanto region. The Tachikawa Disaster Base will serve as the central hub for emergency operations, concentrating mainly on the distribution of manpower and relief supplies by air transport. The base also serves as a disaster awareness and preparedness educational facility for citizens.[1]

In the event of a large-scale disaster, the national government will establish a disaster response headquarters. The headquarters will be set up in the Crisis Management Center (Kiki Kanri Sentaa), located in the Prime Minister's Office (Kantei). If the Prime Minister's Office is unable to be used for any reason, the headquarters will be moved to the Cabinet Office's Central Government Building, No. 5 (Chūō Gōdō Chōsha Gogōkan), a little more than one kilometer away to the east. If both locations are damaged, the headquarters will be moved to the Defense Agency, now ministry, in Ichigaya, several kilometers away. However, if all locations in the metropolis become dysfunctional, the headquarters will be established at the Tachikawa Disaster Prevention Government Building (Tachikawa Bōsai Gōdō Chōsha). The latter building is equipped with its own generator and water-distilling equipment so that five hundred people can work there for one week with no outside water or electricity.

The Tachikawa Disaster Base is built on approximately 115 hectares of land. The Showa National Memorial Park (Shōwa Kinen Kōen), commercial lands, main highways, and other areas may be turned over in times of a disaster, giving the base a total of 446 hectares of land.

The following facilities are found at the Tachikawa Disaster Base:

> Disaster Headquarters Reserve Facilities (Tachikawa Disaster Prevention Government Building, Cabinet Office Disaster Headquarter Reserve Facilities, and the Kobu Government Building of the Ministry of Land, Infrastructure, and Transport) — a backup facility to command emergency operations.
> Police Disaster Task Force Facility (Keisatsu Bōsai Kankei Shisetsu) (Tokyo Metropolitan Police Department Tama General Government Building, Fourth Riot Control Police, Tokyo Metropolitan Police Department Tama Storage Facility, Tokyo Metropolitan

Police Department Tachikawa Aviation Center, Tokyo Metro-politan Police Department Tachikawa Police Station)—facilities that will serve as a hub for relief operations for helicopter-related functions.

Maritime Disaster-Related Facilities (Japan Coast Guard Agency Coast Guard Experimentation and Research Center [Kaijō Hoanchō Kaijō Hoan Shiken Kenkyū Sentaa])—a facility for aircraft in a disaster.

Fire Disaster–Related Facilities (Tokyo Fire Department Tachikawa Government Building [Tōkyō Shōbōchō Tachikawa Gōdō Chōsha], Tokyo Fire Department Eighth District Training Center [Tōkyō Shōbōchō Dai Hachi Shōbō Hōmen Kunren Sentaa], Tokyo Fire Department Aviation Unit Tama Aviation Center [Tōkyō Shōbōchō Kōkūtai Tama Kōkū Sentaa], Tachikawa Metropolitan Life Safety Learning Center [Tachikawa Tomin Bōsai Kyōiku Sentaa])—facilities to allow for the gathering of emergency information and serving as a key center for com-mands; also possesses helicopter-related facilities.

Self-Defense Forces Aviation-Related Facilities (GSDF Eastern Army Aviation Group, Camp Tachikawa)—airfield to allow for the gathering of emergency information and the undertaking of relief operations during a disaster.

Medical Facilities (National Disaster Medical Center [Dokuritsu Gyōsei Hōjin Kokuritsu Byōin Kikō Saigai Iryō Sentaa])— facility that functions as a hospital in disasters and can undertake special screening and provide medical staff.

Tokyo Tachikawa Disaster Prevention Center—gathers informa-tion; coordinates, stores, and transports relief supplies; and provides staff.

Japan Red Cross–Related Facilities (West Tokyo Metropolitan Red Cross Blood Center [Tōkyōto Nishi Sekijūji Ketsueki Sentaa] and Japan Red Cross Society Tokyo Chapter Disaster Relief Storage Site [Nihon Seikijūjisha Tōkyō Shibu Saigai Kyūgo Sōko])—blood products and facilities to provide to medical professionals; facilities for relief measures and storage of sup-plies in a disaster.

Food Storage Facilities (Ministry of Agriculture, Forestry, and Fisheries Tokyo Agricultural Administration Office, Tachikawa Government Storage Site [Nōrin Suisanshō Tōkyō Nōsei Jimusho Tachikawa Seifu Sōko])—storage area for rice, bread, and other dry food products for use during a disaster.

Living Quarters (quarters for workers preparing for disasters and in time of disasters)—these quarters allow officials to respond in the first stages following a disaster by having them there on a twenty-four-hour basis.

A GSDF runway is located to the west of the Tachikawa Disaster Base at Camp Tachikawa, making air transportation possible.[2] There will likely be many casualties instantly if a large earthquake directly strikes Tokyo. Due to the unprecedented circumstances, the prime minister, Japan's supreme commander in chief, could become unable to carry out his duties. A 1999 reform of the Cabinet Law (Naikakuhō) determines how the powers of the prime minister would be transferred in the event the prime minister were unavailable or unable to carry out his duties.

Article 9: Should anything happen to the prime minister or if the prime minister is disabled, the predetermined minister of state will take the office of the prime minister immediately.

Article 10: If anything happens to the chief minister of state or if the chief minister of state is disabled, the predetermined minister of state will take the office of the prime minister immediately.

In the United States of America, the vice president automatically takes the office of the president if the latter is unable to carry out his duties as president. If the vice president is incapable of taking office, the order of appointment to the commander-in-chief's office is determined by law. However, Japan does not have an official position of deputy prime minister or vice prime minister. Instead the procedures are to predetermine the appointment of five ministers who would replace the prime minister at a time of emergency. In principle the chief Cabinet secretary is the first to succeed the prime minister. The other four candidates are selected based on their position, personal experiences, and the like.

The Cabinet Office Information Integration Center (Naikaku Jōhō Shūyaku Sentaa) was established in 1996 to strengthen crisis management capabilities. Here 140 employees are on duty twenty-four hours a day. Half of the employees are dispatched from the National Police Agency, the Public Safety Intelligence Agency (Kōan Chōsachō), the Coast Guard, and the Ministry of Finance.

The following introduces the state of communications with Cabinet members in ordinary times and how the members would assemble in an emergency.

Assembling when a state of emergency is issued
(November 21, 2003, Cabinet Understanding)

I. Preparing for a state of emergency
  A. Prepare for a state of emergency by being able to be reached at all times and understanding the communication routes within each ministry.
  B. (Not included here by author.)
  C. Predetermine the transportation route and assembly route to each ministry and to the Prime Minister's Office, as in an emergency it will be necessary for officials to get to the predetermined assembly point. Every ministry should anticipate that it may be disconnected from one's secretary and police protection. Know where the closest police station is.
II. (Not included here by author.)
III. (Not included here by author.)
IV. Responding to a direct hit, large-scale earthquake in Tokyo
  A. If there is seismic intensity of level 6 or higher within the twenty-three districts of Tokyo, the Prime Minister's Office Crisis Management Center will be the assembly point for each minister. If the Crisis Management Center is disabled, the prime minister or the chief Cabinet minister will decide the next assembly point according to the situation:

1. Cabinet Office (Central Government Office Building No. 5)
2. Defense Agency [Ministry]
3. Tachikawa Disaster Base (Disaster Headquarters Reserve Facility)

    In a situation in which the assembly point is not clearly established, each minister is to go to his or her respective ministry.

B. (Not included here by author.)
C. The transportation method for assembly is as follows:
1. Each minister is to use all possible methods to assemble at the determined location.
2. Plan to use police cars or other emergency vehicles to assembly point if transportation by road is permitted.
3. Check beforehand for possible helicopter landing zones near the private homes of the prime minister, prime minister replacement candidates, chief Cabinet minister, or minister of disaster prevention in case transportation by road is impossible.

Basically these instructions mean that each minister is on duty twenty-four hours a day. It would probably be best to place a GPS bracelet on each minister.

But we do not know when an earthquake will strike. It could happen while one is driving on the road or while one is on vacation. It is important to have measures in place that will allow one to be able to respond to any situation at any time.

In Tokyo employees are on duty twenty-four hours a day at the Tokyo Disaster Prevention Center, located on the ninth floor of City Office Building No. 1 in Shinjuku. There are also 210 apartments near the Tokyo Disaster Prevention Center and 65 apartments at the Tachikawa Disaster Base to accommodate the staff at the Disaster Prevention Center. Once a state of emergency is issued, staff living in these quarters immediately assemble and go into full operational mode. Also all employees of the Tokyo government are required to assemble at their designated locations without needing to await orders.

Ten year after the Kobe earthquake, the *Sankei Shimbun* did a story on disaster preparation in Tokyo, looking at the role of one individual in particular:

> Director of Crisis Management Nakamura Masahiko sleeps watching the Tokyo Metropolitan Government Building every night. Housing complexes that are designed to withstand earthquakes and disasters are built around the Tokyo Metropolitan Government Building. Two hundred disaster-prevention agency employees live in these housing complexes away from their families. Director Nakamura is one of them. The position of crisis management director was established in 2004 to direct specific operations in case of terrorism or great earthquakes. If a crisis occurs, the director gathers information on the situation from all districts, cities, towns, and villages from the Tokyo Metropolitan Government Building. The director then decides on whether to dispatch the Tokyo Metropolitan Police Department, Tokyo Fire Department's rescue division, and the Self-Defense Forces. The Tokyo Metropolitan Government's disaster management plan is based on the assumption of a magnitude 7.2 inland Tokyo earthquake. The estimated death toll is 7,159 people and 158,000 injuries. The estimated death toll and injuries are larger than those in the Great Hanshin-Awaji disaster. Director Nakamura carries four different communication devices with him at all times, including two cell phones and a wireless radio for times of crisis. In the last two years he has been back to his home only for three days in total. He can only take a walk within thirty minutes of his office. Nakamura says, "I am ready for anything to happen. I am ready for the phone call. I am ready for any disaster."[3]

Director Nakamura is allowed to venture only within a thirty-minute distance of his office in order to be able to run back to his office on foot even if all traffic has stopped due to a crisis. From there he can lead his team and give out the appropriate commands.

But in the time of a real disaster the director may be forced to take detours because of collapsed buildings, lines of cars in accidents, and fires breaking out. On top of this, the director himself may find himself in a situation where he gets hurt or is involved in some sort of accident. This can happen to government officials and other personnel working in disaster management. At 5:00 p.m. on Saturday, July 23, 2005, a seismic intensity-level 5 earthquake struck Tokyo. Calls were made to thirty-four employees on duty at the disaster management housing complex. However, only thirteen out of the thirty-four showed up at the office. Perhaps it is every person for him- or herself when a crisis strikes.

Being Able to Rely on the Self-Defense Forces

The reader is probably familiar with the expression "the golden 72 hours." In the Great Hanshin-Awaji Earthquake 1,100 people were rescued on the first day. They represented 74 percent of the people found that day. On the second day, January 18, 154 people—26.5 percent of those found—were rescued, considerably lower than the day before. On January 19, the third day, 92 were rescued, which corresponds to 19.5 percent of those found. These figures mean that the survival rate of people who were trapped under the debris of collapsed buildings and infrastructure dropped dramatically with each passing day. If rescue operations are conducted immediately, it is very clear that the chance to save the lives of those found goes up.

The GSDF unit that is in charge of disaster response and protection for Kobe City is the Third Artillery Unit (Daisan Tokka Rentai), located in Himeji City, about forty kilometers to the west of Kobe. During the Great Hanshin-Awaji Earthquake detailed information about the scope of the disaster still had not found its way to the GSDF's higher headquarters, Middle Army HQ (Chūbu Hōmentai Sōkanbu), located in Itami City, to Kobe's east, even after 6:30 a.m. The Hyogo Prefecture Government (Hyōgo Kenchō), along with the Hyogo Prefecture Police (Hyōgoken Keisatsu Honbu), could not get hold of the SDF, even by radios used especially for disasters. It was 11:00 a.m., more than four hours after the earthquake had struck, before the governor of Hyogo Prefecture requested the SDF to deploy.

When asked in a variety of television news interviews, the victims of the Great Hanshin-Awaji Earthquake answered that the people they most relied on first were their neighbors, followed by SDF personnel. The SDF can mobilize large trucks, helicopters, and heavy equipment, as well as tens, if not hundreds, of well-organized troops. Moreover, not only can the SDF help search for survivors, but they also can deliver quite a bit of water and food. They even made outdoor baths for the victims of the disaster. However, the SDF's deployment during the time of the Great Hanshin-Awaji Earthquake was not exactly smooth.

The SDF is utilized in the following ways during a disaster:

1. Relief support to disaster areas in typhoons, storms/floods, earthquakes, etc.
2. Search and rescue for survivors in aviation accidents and shipwrecks
3. Transportation of emergency cases
4. Provision of water to arid areas or areas where water service has been affected
5. Fighting of wildfires

However, the dispatch of the SDF is quite troublesome. According to the *Defense of Japan* (*Bōei hakusho*), the white paper of the then Japanese Defense Agency,

> As far as disaster relief dispatches are concerned, the SDF makes it a principle to carry out requests by prefectural governors and other officials as stipulated in Article 83 of the Self-Defense Forces Law [Jieitaihō]. This arrangement is such that the prefectural governors and other officials assume primary responsibility for disaster countermeasures, and it is grounded in the concept that it is the most appropriate for the Defense Agency to arrive at a decision on whether to dispatch the SDF in response to requests by prefectural governors and other officials since they are in a position to grasp the overall picture of the circumstances of the disaster.[4]

According to Paragraph 2, Article 68, of the Disaster Measures Basic Law, the mayor of a city, town, or village can ask the governor of his or her prefecture to request the dispatch of the SDF for disaster relief. However, in emergency cases when the governor cannot be reached,—such as when he or she is traveling abroad or his or her location is unknown due to an accident or other unforeseen circumstance, "the city, town, or village mayor can . . . inform the director general of the Defense Agency or an official he designates about the situation in the affected area. In this situation, when there is no time to wait for a request to be made, the director general of the Defense Agency or his appointed official can order the SDF to undertake the necessary relief operations to protect life and property." This is an example of the so-called self-ordering or independent dispatch (*jishu haken*).

However, there is a proviso in Paragraph 2, Article 83, of the Self-Defense Forces Law that mentions the following in the context of disaster relief dispatches: "[The SDF can act] when judged necessary in order to protect lives and property . . . in the event of an act of God or other disaster . . . [in] particularly urgent situations when it is deemed there is no time to wait for a request to be made."

While the above is quite complicated, the essence of it seems to be that the SDF can decide on their own to deploy when a situation is so serious that they cannot wait for a request to come from the governor or other officials charged with making such a request. This is something that the victims in a disaster also understand.

The Disaster Measures Basic Law was revised in December 1995. In a large-scale disaster the Emergency Disaster Measures Headquarters (Kinkyū Saigai Taisaku Honbu), which is comprised of all of the Cabinet members, can meet even if the prime minister has not declared a disaster. Through this revision of the law, the SDF can legally respond more rapidly to provide relief in disasters.

In other words, the basis for the dispatch of the SDF without a request by a governor was clarified. When aerial surveillance and the gathering of intelligence are necessary to respond, for earthquakes over magnitude 5 on the Richter Scale, the SDF can automatically deploy its units. Moreover, if it has become technologically impossible to communicate with a governor, the SDF can deploy on their own, thereby making their response to a natural disaster much more flexible.

For this reason the Defense Agency has asked all of the local governments to include the following items in their disaster plans:

1. The securing of hubs for supplies
2. The securing of heliports
3. The designation of numbers on the roofs of buildings for use in the gathering of information by aircraft and the transporting of personnel and supplies

These are all things learned in the wake of the Great Hanshin-Awaji Earthquake.

Following the December 2004 Sumatra earthquake, the United States immediately dispatched sixteen thousand personnel to the affected countries around the Indian Ocean. Twenty-one ships, including the aircraft carrier USS *Abraham Lincoln* and the multipurpose amphibious assault ship USS *Bonhomme Richard*, were sent to the area and conducted operations from the sea in which food, water, and medical supplies were delivered to the disaster area with minimum impact on the local infrastructure.[5] The distribution of water began in full on January 3.

The response of the SDF, on the other hand, went as follows after the December 26 Sumatra earthquake. On December 28 the Defense Agency sent an official to the region, but the rest of the Japanese government agencies closed for the holidays on this day. By January 1, 2005, a plan was developed to send one thousand SDF personnel to the region. No efforts or involvement by Japan's politicians or bureaucrats were seen. On January 3 the Indonesian government officially requested support from the world community. On January 4 the SDF was issued an order to prepare to deploy. It was not until the end of January before the SDF was able to fully begin to undertake relief operations.[6]

In contrast, the Australian Army engineers deployed on December 31 with helicopters and bulldozers aboard the HMAS *Kanimbla*, a landing platform amphibious ship, and by January 3, as with the U.S. military, they were fully supplying water to the disaster area.

In addition, Germany, the Netherlands, France, Russia, and others had all sent in ground forces by the middle of January. On December 27 the French foreign minister had traveled on a government airplane to the disaster area along with sixty rescue personnel. Of course it has to be remembered that more than five thousand French citizens were vacationing in the area when the disaster occurred, and thus France had a strong interest in what had happened there.

The delay in dispatching the SDF was less a problem of the SDF than it was a political failure. Japan must be able to respond more quickly to disasters. This is particularly true when we consider the fact that the SDF has to wait for a request from the governors in a disaster area before fully responding.

The Necessity for the Speedy Transmission of Information

The following is a minute-by-minute timeline of the response, or lack thereof, on the day of the Great Hanshin-Awaji Earthquake of January 17, 1995, based on reporting from one of the national newspapers and compiled into a book with photos from that time:[7]

5:46   Earthquake strikes.

6:00   A fax that reads, "Earthquake strikes the Kinki region," is sent to the office of Kunimatsu Koji, commissioner general of the National Police Agency.

6:30   Emergency call is made to Middle Army Headquarters of the GSDF.

6:30   Kobe mayor Sasayama Kazutoshi arrives at the city offices wearing sneakers and sweatpants.

6:30   National Police Agency establishes an earthquake disaster management office (*hishin saigai taisakushitsu*) within its HQ building in Tokyo and orders dispatch of task forces from Osaka, Kyoto, and Nara.

6:40   Hyogo Prefecture Disaster Management Headquarters (Hyōgoken Saigai Taisaku Honbu) established.

6:50   Kobe City Disaster Management Headquarters (Kōbeshi Saigai Taisaku Honbu) established.

7:30   Prime Minister Murayama Tomiichi receives first word about earthquake from secretary at his official residence.

7:30   GSDF dispatches a unit of fifty soldiers from Itami.

8:00   SDF helicopters fly over the disaster-stricken region assessing damage.

8:00   Two hundred and fifty-four GSDF troops are dispatched from Camp Itami to the site of destroyed housing districts around Hankyu Itami Train Station and Nishinomiya City.

8:45   Prime minister releases following comment to press: "We are doing our best, working hard to grasp the situation. Currently we are working to take measures to respond to this disaster."

9:00   Hyogo Prefecture governor Kaihara Toshitami arrives at the prefectural office.

9:19   Prime Minister Murayama goes to his office. "The damage appears to be growing. We need to begin thinking about establishing an emergency disaster management headquarters. I am going to dispatch the director general of the National Land Agency (Kokudochō) now."

9:55   National Police Agency publicizes first disaster reports: "As of 9:50 this morning, 222 people have died and 223 people are buried alive in Hyogo Prefecture."

10:00   Hyogo Prefecture governor Kaihara requests the deployment of the SDF; four hundred troops are dispatched from Camp Himeji.

10:00   Fire and Disaster Management Agency Disaster Response Headquarters (Shōbōchō Saigai Taisaku Honbu) requests the Osaka Fire Department and Tokyo Fire Department to lend support.

10:04   Cabinet decision is made to establish the 1995 Southern Hyogo Prefecture Earthquake Response Headquarters (Heisei 7 Nen Hyōgoken Nanbu Jishin Hijō Saigai Taisaku Honbu), headed by director general of National Land Agency.

10:35   Fire and Disaster Management Agency orders the deployment of firefighters from Tokyo, Chiba, Yokohama, Kawasaki, Nagoya, Hiroshima, and Fukuoka.

10:45   Minister of International Trade and Industry Hashimoto Ryutaro holds a press conference during which he states, "I am worried about the effect [the disaster will have] on small and medium businesses. We still do not know if gas, electricity, and other lifelines have been affected."

10:50   Minister of Home Affairs Nonaku Hiromu holds a conference with various ministries. He says, "The police department has deployed over seven hundred officers from Shikoku, Chugoku, and Kinki, but they are having a difficult time on the roads with all of the closures."

11:00   Kyoto Police Task Force arrives in Hyogo Prefecture.

12:00   Establishment of the Southern Hyogo Prefecture Earthquake Response Headquarters, headed by director general of National Land Agency.

12:00 Ministry of Economy, Trade, and Industry orders Kansai Electric Power Company (Kansai Denryoku) to take necessary measures to help with relief efforts.

12:06 Prime Minister Murayama grieves as he is told that the death toll has gone beyond two hundred people during Heads of Ruling Parties Liaison Meeting (Seifu Yotō Shunō Renraku Kaigi).

12:30 Director of Fire and Disaster Management Agency leaves for Kobe City

12:48 Three SDF helicopters land next to the Ichimiya-cho Town Office, Awaji Island. Troops begin damage assessment using motorcycles.

13:00 The Ministry of Transport Bureau of Aeronautics (Unyushō Kōkukyoku) orders three commercial airline companies to run emergency flights because land transportation has been shut down.

13:10 Two hundred fifteen members of the GSDF Third Artillery Unit, begin rescue missions.

15:05 Prime Minister Murayama calls for emergency conference to discuss disaster management. He orders Fire and Disaster Management Agency director Taki Makoto, who is on site, to "increase efforts toward rescuing those who are trapped and buried alive under rubble."

16:00 Prime Minister Murayama holds emergency press conference. There are no specific plans yet, and the government is not responding quickly enough.

17:00 Osaka Coast Guard director orders a patrol boat to send rescue relief to Awaji Island.

18:20 Director general of National Land Agency, Ozawa Kiyoshi, arrives at Hyogo Prefecture Government Building and is shocked when he is told that the death toll is over one thousand.

18:30 Ministry of Trade, Economy, and Industry requests that various industries secure emergency goods such as blankets, gas stoves, and kerosene.

20:30 Eight hundred twenty officers and police rescue units from Kinki, Chugoku, and Shikoku Police Departments arrive at Nishinomiya Police Station.

21:00 Fifty-three firefighters from Osaka Fire Department leave for Kobe on two ships, the *Namihaya* and the *Takatsu*, carrying bread and food for nine thousand people and 2.4 tons of drinking water.

22:15 Ashiya City mayor Kitamura Harue in telephone call to Osaka City Fire Department requests support, stating, "We do not have enough ambulances."

The above is a portion of government and other records from the time the Southern Hyogo Prefecture Earthquake struck on January 17, 1995, until the end of the first day. By 6:00 a.m. the next morning, 2,300 GSDF troops were on rescue relief missions. By 19:00 that evening the number of troops had increased to 9,500. In addition, ninety-four commercial airplanes were used to transport goods to the disaster site.

Relief operations after a disaster are a race against time. Where there are victims seeking help, there are others working hard to get to those in need of help. Hundreds or thousands of people's lives may be lost if decisions are delayed even for a minute. Specific information is necessary to make the right decisions. For these, a system that gathers vital information efficiently and transmits this information effectively is key. It is important, also, to be constantly aware of the danger of disasters and to regularly prepare for them.

During the Great Hanshin-Awaji Earthquake none of this was done. Nobody thought that a disaster of this scale would strike the region. Now that we know that the unexpected can happen, it is urgent to create a system that can help save people's lives as soon as possible.

Preventing the Loss of Data

According to the Japanese IT and business website Japan.Internet .com,

> On December 24, 2004, Kanbara Town in Shizuoka Prefecture and TKC Corporation announced that they conducted backup data recovery training by creating a backup data server in a remote location using IP-VAN in anticipation of a large-scale disaster. The training tested the procedures and time it takes for the office functions to be fully operational after a disaster and the reliability of the data that have been automatically backed up by the "TKC administration ASP/2nd Backup Services." The test found that "All of the citizens' data, including the transfer data input immediately before the assumed disaster, were fully recovered." "It is possible for an office or a business to function with the restoration of backup data after a disaster strikes." The

results were good enough for Kanbara Town to use for its own disaster preparation measures, and TKC can now use its knowledge to better the TKC Administration ASP/2nd Backup Services. This system automatically backs up data that are routed by the TKC Internet service center via LGWAN networks. The cities, towns, and villages that use this service will have the data of residents automatically stored in a remote server. Data backed up in the TISC will make it possible for the administrative offices to recover and gather information in case the disaster destroys their buildings or information system. TKC has also created the "e-TASK series" which is its general administrative information system.[8]

It is safe to say that modern businesses revolve around information. What would happen if their data were lost?

The movement to protect data stored in computers from disasters is spreading widely from local administrations to businesses. Businesses that have the financial capability to do so possess the power of a computer similar to their main computer as a backup in a remote location. New data and information are periodically input in preparation for a disaster. Even if the main computer is destroyed by an earthquake, they can switch to their backup computer and resume business. To make it cost effective, some businesses divide and store their data in different remote servers.

For example, what if the Ministry of Finance's computer were damaged and all of the data were lost? Japan's economy would become chaotic and may not be able to function. If data were lost from the Social Insurance Agency (Shakai Hokenchō), all data related to national pensions would be lost.[9] It is possible to lose information about past pension payments and lose all of the data stored. What would happen if police departments' data were lost from their computers? It is the same for banks and securities companies.

Following an earthquake, damaged computers will be thrown away and scrapped. It is important to keep in mind that information can still leak from these discarded computers. The government stores a lot of important information about its citizens. Mass chaos is imminent if the data are destroyed or get into the wrong hands.

Business Measures against Earthquakes

"A city you can run to instead of run away from." This is the catch-phrase of the fifty-four-story office building called Roppongi Hills in the upscale Roppongi area of Tokyo. Roppongi Hills is designed to withstand earthquakes of seismic intensity level 7 and even has its own electric generator. Many businesses that seek safety sign a lease for a unit in this building.

According to 2002 data, 20 percent of the businesses in the country had a "business continuity" plan after a disaster, 70 percent had only one main computer, and 50 percent had a backup computer. Only 60 percent had a disaster protocol, and only 40 percent had verified their building's earthquake resistance. In recent years there have been many debates over when the next large earthquake directly beneath Tokyo and a Tokai earthquake will strike. Because of this, business consciousness toward such threats has increased, and businesses have begun to take measures in preparation for such disasters.

If a Tokai, Tonankai, and Nankai earthquake all strike at the same time, the entire length of one thousand kilometers from the Izu Peninsula to Cape Ashizuri in Shikoku will be hit by seismic intensity level 5 to 6, and all of the coastlines will be threatened by tsunamis. Many of Japan's key industries are situated along the Pacific Belt.

Toyota has three subsidiary factories in Japan and forty-five overseas production plants in twenty-six different countries in North America, South America, Europe, and Asia. All of Toyota's accounting, production, and parts distribution is managed by Toyota's main computer in Aichi Prefecture. After an earthquake, even if the computer can be restored using the data on the backup system, if the plants that produce parts cease to function, it is possible that Toyota's entire production worldwide will come to a halt. Similarly Toyota has plants in Argentina, Australia, and the Republic of South Africa, and if production comes to a halt, it will literally mean that the effects of the disaster will have reached to the other side of the globe.

If factories and transportation routes cease to function for industries that manage resources, parts production, and final products in factories in Japan and overseas, it will directly affect factories that are not in a disaster-stricken region. It is necessary to have an overall system of measures hedging against disasters for industries in both the production and distribution sectors.

In some companies employees are sent home if a Tokai earthquake warning is issued. If an earthquake strikes during off-duty hours, companies will check on the safety of their employees by cell phone text messages and other means. Also procedures for responding to the disaster are pre-decided. In the financial sector offices are equipped with generators for electricity and a backup system. They even have a manual for the speedy reopening of their business.

On September 11, 2001, the World Trade Center in New York, America's economic symbol, collapsed as a result of a terrorist attacks, and there were many victims. This was not simply a loss of many lives and the destruction of the Twin Towers, but also the destruction of information of the businesses in the building. All of the businesses' computers were buried under the debris and rubble. Even then, however, some businesses were able to recover and restart their operations rather quickly. These were the businesses that had backup computers in remote facilities. Some banks had a system that automatically backed up data to a computer that was over ten kilometers away.

The Japanese telephone company, KDDI, announced in June 2005 that "[it was reintroducing] 'Iridium' satellite cell phone services effective June 1 after having halted its services for five years. The retail price [for such a phone service] is set at 241,500 yen [$2,415], but it can also be rented for about 25,000 yen [$250] a week."[10]

"Iridium" can make phone calls from anywhere in the world using satellites, but KDDI had stopped its service for a while until recently. Local administrations and businesses are now reevaluating "Iridium" for use during emergency situations such as earthquakes or other large disasters. Financial institutions in Japan are now applying the lessons learned from the Great Hanshin-Awaji Earthquake, setting up satellite cell phones in important hubs in Tokyo, Osaka, and Kobe. They have also established remote computer systems outside of Tokyo and Osaka, protecting their information and speeding up the restitution of services. A data center server that is earthquake proof and theft proof was created in the Kanto region.

In the imminent threat of a large-scale disaster that may strike Japan any time, it is necessary to begin considering the establishment of backup data facilities. It is possible for both Tokyo and Osaka to be crippled by a disaster.

A railway company in the Kinki region has a manual in case of a tsunami. Trains that run in areas under intensified measures against earthquake disasters are required to stop at the nearest station once an earthquake warning is issued. If the nearest train station is unmanned or is along the coast where a tsunami is expect to hit, the conductor is required to go to a station that is on high ground and then help evacuees.

There may be earthquake maps at facilities that people frequent, such as department stores, baseball stadiums, movie theaters, and theaters, but like tsunami hazard maps, the government and experts should invest the time and money to create such emergency maps where they do not exist. It would be more efficient if such maps were distributed to the facility managers and they decided which route was the most suitable in each situation. If protocols are created by someone who has no expertise or no local knowledge, they could cause more damage and needlessly endanger people. The nation, prefectures, cities, towns, villages, and public all need to cooperate and prepare for a future disaster.

But are the essential government administrations prepared for disasters? As of 2005 of the eleven central government office buildings in the Kasumigaseki area of Tokyo, five buildings of the Ministry of Finance and the Cabinet Office did not meet the earthquake resistance standards. Also unofficial government reports found that 4 percent of the 335 electronic pieces of data crucial during a disaster are not protected under any safety measures and that 7 percent of the backup computer systems are stored in the same location as the main computer. This is unacceptable, as the government itself needs to lead and guide the public during a time of disaster.

Survival

We cannot, however, rely exclusively on the government. It is critical that we, as individuals, be aware and prepared rather than depending on the government or local administrations in regard to megaquakes.

There are many things we can do on an everyday basis—keeping bathtubs filled with water daily, for one. If you do not want to walk barefoot on glass and rubble, keep a pair of shoes or slippers near your bed. Have your checkbook and cash ready next to your bed. Maintain a minimum three-day supply of water and food, as well as a supply of flashlights, batteries, and radios in order to get through the early stages of a disaster.

It is important to know to turn off all of the gas lines, shut off the breakers, and open the doors when an earthquake hits. Aftershocks could make it impossible for doors to open. If the stove was left on before evacuation and the electricity gets turned back on and there is no one in the house, it could cause a fire. A tenth or even half of the damage from disasters can be reduced by these small but important actions.

Local administrations across Japan have exhibits and learning centers for disaster prevention from earthquakes, fires, and floods. There one can experience the force of an earthquake of different seismic levels, learn how to navigate through smoke, apply emergency first aid, use a fire extinguisher, and receive basic information for disaster prevention. In Kobe at such a center, I was able to hold a fire hose during a drill and was deeply impressed with its intensity. Since the Great Hanshin-Awaji Earthquake we have learned many lessons, and our awareness toward disasters has increased. Many books have been written on disaster prevention, disaster reduction, and disaster mitigation as well.

However, the precautions mentioned above are useful only if you survive the first hit from an earthquake. A report by the Hyogo Prefecture Medical Observatory Office (Hyōgoken Kansatsu Imushitsu) of deaths in Kobe City during the Great Hanshin-Awaji Earthquake stated, "Over 90 percent [of the deaths] occurred within fifteen minutes after the first earthquake." Almost all of the 90 percent died due to being crushed by buildings or suffocating. In other words, people do not die from the shaking caused by an earthquake. People die under collapsed houses, being crushed by furniture, and suffocating from being buried under rubble. Fire is the other half of the cause of the deaths.

During the Great Hanshin-Awaji Earthquake about 240,000 buildings that did not meet earthquake resistance standards were fully or partially destroyed, and about 5,500 people lost their lives immediately after the earthquake. The cost of damage to buildings was close to 6 trillion yen ($60 billion). Most of these buildings were apartment complexes, condominiums, and buildings designed under the former standards for disaster resistance. Earthquake resistance in buildings is extremely important.

The most important thing during an earthquake is to survive the initial quake. No matter how prepared you are or what degree of survival skills you have, if you die, then that is it. Even if you have only the shirt on your back, if you survive, things will work out somehow later. Relief goods, aid, and volunteers will come from all over Japan. There have been many earthquakes in recent years, but there has been no news of people dying of starvation at the shelters. There is enough food as long as you don't expect a luxurious life. Even if you cannot eat or drink for a day, you should at least appreciate the fact that you are still alive.

To survive an earthquake, first you must live in a house that will not collapse, and you must prevent fires at all costs. It is best to build a house on a strong foundation or even rebuild your home to make it resistant to earthquakes, but this might not be possible for some people. However, reinforcing your house, securing furniture, and clarifying evacuation routes are possible. Small changes like finding a safer room in which to sleep or changing the position of your bed could even make the difference between life and death during an earthquake. However, most people do not think that they will die or lose their homes from an earthquake. That is why some can live carelessly in houses that are not built on firm ground or not spend any money toward earthquake resistance even when they have the money to do so.

If you choose to live in such a house or not make the changes suggested above, it will be too late when an earthquake hits if your house collapses or you are killed somehow. If you survive, then you should thank God that you are still alive. For earthquakes it is important how you have prepared ahead of time instead of during or after.

As discussed in chapter 2, fraudulent statements regarding the structural designs of condominiums and hotels were discovered in 2005. It was discovered that many condominiums and hotels lacked steel reinforcement and were likely to collapse if an earthquake over seismic intensity level 5 struck. In this set of scandals the words "having to do with life" or, more exactly, "one's life depends on it" (*inochi ni kakawaru*) were frequently used, and it is exactly that: a safe home or building is a matter of life or death. A lot of people must have reevaluated the importance of earthquake resistance when considering the value of a home or building instead of simply noting its appearance, space, and location. The Ministry of Land, Infrastructure, and Transport found in 2004 that 30–40 percent of the buildings in Japan did not meet earthquake resistance standards and were unfit. The Japan Wood House Earthquake Resistance and Reinforcement Union (Nihon Kizō Jūtaku Taishin Hokyō Jigyōsha Kyōdō Kumiai) has found that 60 percent of wooden houses built after 1981 are in danger of collapsing in the event of an earthquake. It also found that if an earthquake of seismic intensity level 5 or higher struck, 50 percent of the wooden houses would be in danger of complete destruction, and if partial danger of collapse were included, the proportion would rise to 74 percent.

In other words, the number of houses that would be completely destroyed is enormous nationwide if an earthquake of seismic intensity level 5 or higher struck. Old wooden structures would collapse at an even lower-level seismic intensity earthquake. After the discovery of the fraudulent statements of structural design, certain local administrations ordered the evacuation of certain homes. I agree with this policy, but what about the rest of the people who live in houses that are in danger of collapsing from an earthquake of seismic intensity level 5 or lower?

No matter how strong the earthquake resistance is in the house in which you live, when it collapses, it collapses. The true earthquake disaster will start here for those that were lucky enough to survive. At this time the flashlights, food, and water that have been prepared for such an occasion will have no meaning. It is important to be insured by an insurance company that will take care of collapsed houses, burned-down houses, and injuries caused by earthquakes. It is important to have the emotional strength to keep on surviving even if you lose your home, job, or loved ones.

"Home route maps" have become a popular topic within the larger cities. One problem with earthquakes that strike large cities is that millions of people will be stranded and not able to go home. People will begin to fill train stations as the means of transportation stop functioning during earthquakes and typhoons. The "home route maps" indicate all of the hazards and routes one can take to walk to one's house. There is some value in these maps, but the best thing to do is to go to the nearest evacuation shelter and spend a couple of days there until the situation begins to calm down. In the city it is dangerous to walk around after a large earthquake has struck. Buildings can collapse anytime, fires can start, and frequent aftershocks will make it extremely dangerous to move around. You could lose your life, despite having fortunately survived the first earthquake. Walking around could also mean that you could get in the way of the fire department, SDF personnel, and police that are out on rescue missions. I recommend that you stay at an evacuation shelter for a while and help those that are in need there.

Earthquakes, typhoons, volcano eruptions, and heavy rainfall cannot be stopped by humans. There are many natural disasters in Japan. In the future these disasters may be prevented or better predicted with the power of science, but until then all we can do is our best at disaster prevention and disaster reduction. I wonder how seriously people who live in Japan understand such threats. It is important to learn the challenges of natural disasters and to have the proper knowledge from elementary school. It is also important to know the true state of the nation in which we live.

CHAPTER 6

What the Government of Japan Is Doing Now and Should Continue to Do in the Future

Too Many Organizations and Committees

We often see mention of the Central Disaster Management Council, the Headquarters for Earthquake Research Promotion, the Regional Assessment Committee to Strengthen Earthquake and Disaster Measures (Jishin Bōsai Taisaku Kyōka Chiiki Hanteikai), the Coordinating Committee for Earthquake Prediction (Jishin Yochi Renrakukai), and the Coordination Committee of Earthquake Prediction Research (Jishin Yochi Kenkyū Kaigi) in newspapers and on television when there is talk about earthquakes.[1] A brief introduction of each of these organizations follows.

Central Disaster Management Council

The Central Disaster Management Council was established in the Cabinet Office based on the Disaster Measures Basic Law.[2] The head of the council is the prime minister. The council is made up of all of the Cabinet ministers and heads of public organizations (the president of the Bank of Japan [Nihon Ginkō]; the president of the Japan Red Cross Society; the chairman of the Nippon Broadcasting Company [Nihon Hōsō Kyōkai, or NHK]; and the chairman of the Nippon Telegraph and Telephone Corporation [NTT; Nihon Denshin Denwa Kabushiki Kaisha]), and four current scholars or professors emeriti. The council's mission is to formulate basic national disaster plans and decide on important policies for earthquakes, volcanic eruptions, typhoons, and other wind- and water-related disasters.

Headquarters for Earthquake Research Promotion

The headquarters was established based on the Special Law on Earthquake and Disaster Measures, which was passed as a result of the lessons of the Great Hanshin-Awaji Earthquake.[3] At first the headquarters was located within the Prime Minister's Office but now is under the jurisdiction of the Ministry of Education, Culture, Sports, Science, and Technology and is chaired by the minister of that agency. Under the headquarters are two committees—the Policy Committee (Seisaku Iinkai) and the Earthquake Research Committee.

Regional Assessment Committee to Strengthen Earthquake and Disaster Measures

The "Assessment Committee" (Hanteikai), as it is commonly known, is an advisory body to the director general of the Japan Meteorological Agency and was created to be able to predict a Tokai earthquake. If the committee judges an earthquake is imminent based on the results of observations of precursory phenomena and other data, it informs the Cabinet, and an earthquake warning or advisory is announced.

Coordinating Committee for Earthquake Prediction

The Coordinating Committee is an advisory body to the director general of the Geographical Survey Institute (Kokudo Chiriin),[4] which is attached to the Ministry of Land, Infrastructure, Transport, and Tourism (MLIT's new name as of January 2008). Its purpose is to share data on earthquake predictions and research.

Coordination Committee of Earthquake Prediction Research

The committee was created within the Earthquake Research Institute (ERI; Jishin Kenkyūsho) of Tokyo University and is operated by universities from all around the country.[5]

In addition to the aforementioned organizations, there are also other groups conducting studies and research about earthquakes. These include the National Research Institute for Earth Science and

Disaster Prevention (Bōsai Kagaku Gijutsu Kenkyūsho);[6] the Japan Agency for Marine-Earth Science and Technology (Kaiyō Kagaku Gijutsu Sentaa);[7] the Hydrographic and Oceanographic Department of the Japan Coast Guard (Kaijō Hoanchō Kaiyō Jōhōbu); the National Institute of Advanced Industrial Science and Technology;[8] and the (Communications Research Laboratory (CRL; Tsūshin Sōgō Kenkyūsho),[9] among others.

Just how many people in Japan in fact understand how these organizations are structured, how they differ from one another, and how they interface?

First of all, it must be made clear that there are actually no earthquake or volcanic specialists on the Central Disaster Management Council. The council covers all national disasters, including typhoons, floods, and terrorism. It is made up for the most part of politicians and some members of the business community. Thus the actual work of the committee is conducted by disaster specialists who work sort of as subcontractors. Indeed it is easy to get tripped up on the names of some of these groups, such as the "Government's Central Disaster Council Experts Panel on Earthquake Measures for Direct Hits on Capital 'Earthquake Working Group' (headed by Professor So-and-So of Such-and-Such University) . . ." that appear in the media.

It is the Headquarters for Earthquake Research Promotion that does the specialized work regarding earthquakes. As was mentioned above, there are two committees, the Policy Committee and the Earthquake Research Committee, under the headquarters. The Policy Committee is comprised of the leadership of different ministries and agencies of the national government, heads of local governments, and some scholars. It coordinates surveys and research plans on earthquakes and decides the direction of budget allocations and the release of the results of research. In addition, the Policy Committee has an Earthquake Research and Observation Plans Division (Jishin Chōsa Kansoku Keikakubu), which promotes observations and research on earthquakes, diastrophism, and fault lines. It is the support side of the headquarters, with office staff and a budget. The other committee, the Earthquake Research Committee, meets monthly to review and comment on data gathered by the Japan

Meteorological Agency and submitted by universities or other organizations. In effect, it is a group of specialists.

The other groups—namely, the Regional Assessment Committee to Strengthen Earthquake and Disaster Measures and the Coordinating Committee for Earthquake Prediction—are simply advisory bodies, while the Coordination Committee of Earthquake Prediction Research is a group primarily for experts and enthusiasts interested in the subject.

Of course some of the people associated with these organizations may argue that there is a division of labor among them, but even specialists are at a loss about how to explain the differences among some of these groups. Many committee members overlap among the groups, and it would not be incorrect to say that the current situation is the product of stovepiping and turf battles among government agencies and power struggles among academics.

After every large earthquake and disaster, different specialists with their titles from different organizations appear on talk shows and the news saying all sorts of general, sometimes irresponsible, things, such as "This was a type of earthquake never experienced before, so it is hard to say . . ." or "Aftershocks will continue for a while" or "We will have to continue to monitor the situation for some time." Even an amateur can say stuff like this.

It is not too late for someone to stand up and call for the establishment of an earthquake research and countermeasures center that is able to rise above the bureaucratic fray and take a fruitful, productive approach to the study of earthquakes. All research on earthquakes would be concentrated here. It is a particularly necessary organization to have in Japan, as 10 percent of the world's earthquakes occur in this country. Moreover, some 23 percent of the world's earthquakes over magnitude 6 occur in Japan.

Next we explain why we have so many competing organizations, eating up so much of the taxpayers' money.

The Large-Scale Earthquake Countermeasures Act

The Large-Scale Earthquake Countermeasures Law (Daikibo Jishin Taisaku Tokubetsu Sochihō; commonly known as Daishinhō) was passed in June 1978 and went into effect in December that year. This act is based on the premise that we are able to predict earthquakes, and it was meant to mitigate to the greatest extent possible the damage caused by earthquakes. However, the Tokai-type earthquake is the only one that is predictable at this stage.

According to this act, when an earthquake warning is sent out, the Shinkansen lines come to a stop; the expressways close; and banks, department stores, supermarkets, and other facilities shut their doors. Hospitals stop accepting outpatients. Schools close, and children are sent home. Businesses also close and dismiss their employees before public transportation stops. Residents are to be evacuated from dangerous or vulnerable areas, and the SDF prepares to deploy.

In these ways this act has enormous power—essentially the authority of martial law. When an earthquake warning is announced, the functions of cities temporarily stop, causing approximately 200 billion yen ($2 billion) in losses each day. As a result, the authorities have to be very careful in deciding whether to issue an earthquake warning. However, even if an earthquake does not occur, as long as the research has been sound and done correctly, a warning should still be issued to be on the safe side.

There were a lot of calculations by scientists, officials, and politicians involved in the lead-up to the passage of the Large-Scale Earthquake Countermeasures Act. An annotated timeline of some of the significant events prior to the 1978 act follows.

1962 Seismologists finalize recommendations, described as a blueprint, for earthquake prediction. It calls for the careful observation of certain precursors that could help predict earthquakes. As a result of this report, "Earthquake Prediction—Current Status and Action Plan" (Jishin yochi: Sono genjō to suishin keikaku), preparations for earthquake-predicting capabilities, begin in earnest.[10]

1965 The budget for the first Earthquake Prediction Plan (Jishin Yochi Keikaku) is approved. One hundred-seventy billion yen ($1.7 billion) would be spent over five years. In the previous year a major earthquake had struck Niigata Prefecture that killed twenty-six people, caused oil storage tanks to burn for twelve days straight, and saw a prefecture-operated apartment building tip over due to the liquefaction of the reclaimed land below it, and it led to a new focus on disasters in urban areas. From this time the different government ministries—such as the Japan Meteorology Agency and Japan Coast Guard of the Transportation Ministry, the Geographical Survey Institute (Kokudo Chiriin) of the Construction Ministry, the National Institute of Advanced Industrial Science and Technology of the Ministry of International Trade and Industry (Tsusanshō), the Institute of Radio Waves (Denpa Kenkyūsho) of the Ministry of Posts and Telecommunications (Yuseishō), and the Science and Technology Agency (Kagaku Gijutsuchō)—each began to build their own earthquake-related organizations and compete over budgets.

1969   Coordinating Committee for Earthquake Prediction is established as an advisory body to the director general of the Geographical Survey Institute.

1970   Second Earthquake Prediction Plan (Dainiji Jishin Yochi Keikaku) begun.

1973   Magnitude 7.4 earthquake strikes off coast of Nemuro Peninsula (Hokkaido)

1975   Successful prediction of earthquake in Haicheng, China.[11]

1976   A scientist at Tokyo University's School of Science (Rigakubu) suggests the possibility of a Tokai earthquake scenario, causing a national discussion and raising demands for earthquake-prediction capabilities. However, there were differing views among scientists. For example, some said that it was an unmistakable fact that there was a degree of success in predicting the earthquake in China. Therefore, they argued, it could be said that earthquake prediction was possible. In contrast, others pointed out that even if a lot of money were poured into trying to predict a Tokai earthquake, it did not mean that prediction technology would soon make great strides. Nevertheless, the Third Disaster Prediction Plan (Daisanji Jishin Yochi Keikaku) was slightly revised and started.

1978   Large-Scale Earthquake Countermeasures Law goes into effect. At this time as well, the opinions of experts still varied greatly. For example, some said that while earthquake-prediction technology was still in its early stages, scientists and the public nonetheless did not have the luxury to just debate a Tokai earthquake scenario. Observation equipment had to be set up, they noted, in order to continue the research. Others, however, challenged that view and said that instead of too much weight being placed on earthquake prediction, money, people, and time should be spent on dealing with an earthquake itself. Nevertheless, many others continued to press for earthquake-prediction capabilities, arguing that if the technology had existed in the past, they would have undoubtedly been able to predict previous earthquakes, and with this new technology, they would be able to pick up signs of future earthquakes.

1979   Areas that would experience significant damage as a result of an M6 or greater Tokai earthquake and three-meter tsunamis were to be designated Earthquake Disaster-Response Strengthening Districts (Jishin Bōsai Taisaku Kyōka Chiiki). The Assessment Committee was established at this point as an advisory body to the director general of the Japan Meteorological Agency as well.

After the enactment of the Large-Scale Earthquake Counter-measures Law, money for earthquake-prediction research grew dramatically. During the forty years since the original earthquake prediction plan published in 1962, more than 300 billion yen ($3 billion) has been spent. In the early days the minister of transportation was informed that research would be funded in the millions of yen, and for projects the funding would be in the tens of millions of yen. As a result, rather than doing rather boring basic research, organizations applied for funding for observation equipment that was easy to secure, in areas such as detailed earthquake observation and diastrophism. In particular a lot of research money has gone into earthquake prediction on the belief that it is possible to predict a Tokai earthquake.

When I was writing this book in 2005, 1,200 GPS data points throughout the country were helping to capture minute millimeter changes in land-based diastrophism. In addition, sonar recording points had been laid two thousand meters below the ocean for ocean-based diastrophism observation. Moreover, thanks to GPS, the recording points above water are able to monitor changes on the ocean floor to within a degree of accuracy of 5 centimeters. In this way earthquake research is shifting from pure academia to industry, with many observation points being established throughout the country.

With this said, there are researchers who think it is premature to talk about earthquake prediction and have called for a review of the Large-Scale Earthquake Countermeasures Law. Their view is that without an investment in basic research, it will be impossible to gain a reasonable level of success in earthquake prediction.

Japan has no real success story in its past for predicting earthquakes. Any mention of our having been able to predict one has always been after the fact. In any case, I think that funds invested in earthquake-prediction technology and research are not necessarily wasted, but there is much inefficiency in maintaining many similar-looking and -sounding organizations and in spending so much money to simply set up equipment that sends in data.

The Ability to Predict Earthquakes

In 1995 it was said that there was just a 0.4–0.8 percent chance that a large earthquake would occur along the Nojima Fault within thirty years.[12] In fact it was along the Nojima Fault that the Great Hanshin-Awaji Earthquake occurred. Although the probability was less than 1 percent, the earthquake that resulted was very destructive and happened early.

The earthquake frequency, or rate of earthquakes occurring, along the Nojima Fault was once in 1,800–3,000 years, and thus the probability was very low. Despite the probabilities, an earthquake in southern Hyogo Prefecture did occur, causing the Great Hanshin-Awaji Earthquake, and the earthquake that occurred did not follow human estimates. Of course it is probably better not to release these estimates if the reliability level is not high. However, some estimates need to be released, perhaps with the notation that these estimates are for advisory purposes only and should not be entirely relied on, as you may be terribly affected if a disaster does indeed occur.

The Large-Scale Earthquake Countermeasures Law was created based on the assumption that it is possible to predict earthquakes. However, as has been noted above, some seismologists point out that it is not possible at this time scientifically to predict earthquakes.

As mentioned, the one successful example of earthquake prediction occurred in 1975 in the Chinese city of Haicheng in Liaoning

Province, when a magnitude 7.3 quake struck. At 10:00 a.m. on February 4 of that year, an earthquake warning was issued. The Chinese Earthquake Bureau evacuated the residents of a large area and began showing them movies to keep them occupied. During the showing of the second film, at a little after 7:00 p.m., the earthquake struck. Had the people not been evacuated, deaths would have been in the tens of thousands.

Some of the indicators of the earthquake had been observed during the winter months of the previous year: snakes, which should have been hibernating at this point, were seen out and about; the population of mice grew; and cows, pigs, and other farm animals began acting abnormally. In addition, diastrophism, earth magnetic waves, and changes in the level and quality of water in wells were observed.

In contrast, the following year, at the time of the magnitude 7.8 Tangshan Earthquake in Hebei Province, there were many indicators, but no evacuation warning was issued, and according to official statements, 140,000 people died (unofficial estimates ranged from 600,000 to 800,000).

During the week prior to the Sumatra earthquake on December 26, 2004, a great deal of thunder was reported in the vicinity of where the earthquake occurred. This unusual phenomenon was recorded in Japanese radio wave observatories as well. The increase in thunder is said to be the result of radio waves transmitted from the deep underground through changes in the earth's crust. In the September 5, 2004, earthquake off the coast of the Kii Peninsula, radio wave activity 10–50 times stronger than normal was observed in the vicinity of where the earthquake occurred for at least a month before it struck. There were also abnormalities observed at the time of the Great Hanshin-Awaji Earthquake. However, unfortunately, we learned of all of these cases only after the earthquakes occurred.

Through the use of volumetric strain meters, the measurement of changes in the earth's crust using GPS, and the examination of macroscopic anomalies of changes in animal activity, water level and quality, and radio and chemical phenomena, research on earthquake prediction is progressing. However, the fact remains that there has been only one successful case of clearly predicting an earthquake ahead of time, and that was the Haicheng Earthquake.

From Prediction to Disaster Prevention

Following the passing of the Large-Scale Earthquake Countermeasures Law, expectations grew over the ability to predict earthquakes. The government increased its focus on prediction. However, as noted several times in this book, there are many doubts about the ability to predict earthquakes. Nearly thirty years after the establishment of the Large-Scale Earthquake Countermeasures Law, there is yet to be a seismologist who has accurately predicted an earthquake.

Yet regardless of whether earthquakes can be predicted or not, everyone is in agreement that there will certainly be a megaquake in the near future. Even seismologists who doubt that earthquakes can be predicted recognize this point. If a large-scale earthquake is to hit, it is important to reduce the damage to the greatest extent possible. Recently there has been growing attention to disaster prevention and mitigation.[13]

The views of both government officials and the public in Japan completely changed following the Great Hanshin-Awaji Earthquake. It was learned that earthquakes could happen in any part of Japan, wherever and whenever. And if an earthquake were to occur, the destruction could be worse than anyone could predict. It was also learned that you, your family, or your friends could be among the victims. In other words, earthquakes were no longer a problem for someone else to face. They were real and close. This is probably one of the reasons why volunteerism in Japan has taken root.

The government's slow reaction to the Great Hanshin-Awaji Earthquake was apparent to all, and it was intensely criticized. As a result, the government passed many laws, a more rapid response to disasters was called for, and research progressed. The lessons learned were utilized in the 2004 Niigata-Chuetsu Earthquake. The government's response was rapid, and the SDF gathered information by helicopter immediately after the earthquake.

From the perspective of disaster management, the development of the Disaster Information System, or DIS (Jishin Bōsai Jōhō Shisutemu) is being undertaken. The system promotes the early gathering of information from devastated areas and the sharing of information among related organizations, as well as the reduction of destruction as much as possible.

The Cabinet Office is registering information on territory, topography, roadways, administrative agencies, evacuation shelters, and other disaster-related centers in a data base and creating a DIS. Using these data, the DIS helps to prepare the estimates from disaster destruction and supports plans for disaster-response preparations. It will be possible for the government to prepare the best possible response in each stage after an earthquake, such as the early assessment of earthquake damage, immediate response and support, and long-term repair and reconstruction efforts.

This system is being created for the national as well as the prefectural and local levels. In addition, companies are also involved in preparing their own disaster-information systems, not only to protect their own businesses, but also to help their customers with safety management and the aftercare of their products at the time of a disaster, as well as the ability of these customers to get supplied.

What would most people do if a television broadcast suddenly warned that a magnitude 8 earthquake would strike in ten minutes? At most they would gather the few items around them, turn off the stove, and evacuate. This of course is important, especially if your life is saved as a result. However, beyond this, what can be done? If your house collapses, your neighborhood or town burns to the ground, and a tsunami comes, all you can do is stand by and watch. If you had a few hours' warning, you could choose the things you would bring with you and secure furniture and other things in your home. However, if people have an in-between amount of time— between a few minutes and a few hours—probably more people will end up getting killed.

The government has pursued disaster preparations on the assumption that earthquakes are predictable. However, not only scientists but also average citizens question whether it is really possible to predict earthquakes. Of course research on earthquake prediction is important, but it is also important that, parallel to this, the government work closely with the public on disaster mitigation and disaster preparation.

The Sumatra earthquake and tsunami saw more than 220,000 killed and missing. If the residents of the area and the tourists there had had some previous knowledge, deaths may have been reduced to one-tenth or one-twentieth of that figure. If there had been a tsunami warning center and a warning had gone out to the residents of the area to evacuate, even more of the destruction would have been mitigated.

In 2003 the Fire and Disaster Management Agency of the Ministry of Internal Affairs and Communications found that just 50.3 percent of the public buildings, such as schools, gymnasiums, and community centers, had been earthquake-proofed by local authorities. The lowest percentage was found in Tokushima Prefecture (35.1 percent), closely followed by Nagasaki Prefecture (36.5 percent) and Kagawa Prefecture (36.7 percent). The highest was in Shizuoka Prefecture (72.6 percent), followed by Kanagawa Prefecture (71.9 percent) and metropolitan Tokyo (69.7 percent). The relatively high percentages for Shizuoka and Kanagawa Prefectures, which would be affected by a Tokai earthquake scenario, are understandable; the low figures for Kagawa Prefecture, which would experience a Nankai earthquake, are troubling. This assessment is in part the result of the designation of public facilities as evacuation centers, such as public elementary and middle schools and community centers, regardless of whether they have been fortified or not. While a lack of funding is one reason for the failure to fortify the buildings, one could argue that this is budgeting priority. There is a serious problem if the gymnasium or community center to which people evacuate ends up collapsing in an earthquake. The heavily populated Osaka and Hyōgo Prefectures show public building fortification rates of 44.9 percent and 46.4 percent respectively, figures that are below the national average. It is as if they do not expect an earthquake to strike.

Earthquake Preparations by Other Countries

At the time of the Great Hanshin-Awaji Earthquake, it was almost two hours before word of it first reached the Prime Minister's Office.

It was another two hours before the prime minister reached his office. It turns out he did very little, sadly, after he got there.[14] In contrast, about one year prior to this in the Northridge Earthquake that occurred almost around the same time of morning, President William J. Clinton is said to have received his first report just fifteen minutes after the quake struck.[15]

One of the reasons there is such a dramatic difference between the way the U.S. executive branch and the Japanese executive branch were able to handle the response is that at the time of the Northridge Earthquake, a new system called CUBE (Caltech [California Institute of Technology]/USGS [United States Geological Survey] Broadcast of Earthquakes) was being tested in southern California. CUBE was a system that shared information on earthquakes with the media, fire, police, and other civilian organizations.

In 2001 CUBE transitioned into a new system called TriNet, which covers the entire United States. It is a system that provides all different types of information on earthquakes in real time. Minutes after an earthquake occurs, TriNet not only provides information on areas where the earthquake was felt but also prepares a map and shares it with authorities in particularly affected communities.

America is prepared for earthquake occurrences through a computer system that is constantly observing large movements in the earth's crust and monitoring wide areas of earthquake-prone regions.

The American movie *Dante's Peak* is about a volcano eruption in the Pacific Northwest and features an actor playing a scientist with the U.S. Geological Survey. In the United States important information about earthquakes and volcanoes is centered in the USGS. Research is also conducted there. The USGS was established in 1879 and provides biological, seismological, and geographic information to the U.S. government.

In addition, the United States has the Federal Emergency Management Agency as a mobilized force at the time of earthquakes and other disasters. FEMA, as it is commonly known, was previous directly under the president of the United States. Its headquarters is located in Washington DC. It has approximately 2,700 employees, with ten regional headquarters and a budget of $800 million.

FEMA has a great deal of authority in providing relief and recovery and preparing response plans for earthquakes, typhoons, wildfires, tornadoes, and other natural disasters. FEMA is also responsible for dealing with technical and man-made disasters, such as terrorist attacks, nuclear facilities disasters, chemical plant disasters, and gas explosions.

Due to the stovepiping and power struggles that exist in the bureaucracy and universities in Japan, more organizations should not be created, but instead existing ones should be quickly merged into a Japanese version of USGS, and a Japanese version of FEMA should be created that will work closely with the Fire and Disaster Management Agency, the Police Agency, and the SDF. Japan needs to immediately end its bad habits of vested interests and stovepiping. We do not have the luxury of continuing to be indifferent to this problem any longer.

In the report of the tsunami that resulted from the earthquake off of Sumatra, the Hawaii-based Pacific Tsunami Warning Center was often referred to. The center is an organization dedicated to quickly recording earthquakes in the Asia-Pacific region, gathering information about the size and speed of tsunamis that are generated, and sharing that information with member countries.

In May 1960 a magnitude 9.5 trench-type earthquake—the largest in recorded history—struck off the coast of Chile. The resulting tsunami traveled across the Pacific Ocean at a speed of 720 kilometers per hour and spread out. Within twenty-four hours the tsunami reached Japan, on the other side of the earth, and caused death and destruction from Hokkaido all the way to Okinawa. A total of 142 people died or went missing in Japan. As a lesson learned from the Chilean earthquake and tsunami, the United Nations Education, Scientific, and Cultural Organization (UNESCO) created an international monitoring system in 1968. This was the Pacific Tsunami Warning Center, which has been observing and sharing information ever since.

Moreover, in 2004 the French National Center for Space Studies (Centre National d'Études Spatiales) launched a satellite named Demeter. It is part of a project to monitor unusual electrical activity and earth currents and explore the connection with large-scale earthquakes.

Few people would like to live or work in a building that had a sign on it reading, "This building is made out of bricks and is not earthquake resistant. Your safety is not guaranteed in the event of a large earthquake." In the state of California in the United States brick buildings that do not meet earthquake resistance standards are declared structurally weak by local authorities, and their owners are eligible for funds to strengthen the buildings or rebuild them. However, if the building is not made earthquake resistant, the owner is obligated to put up such a sign.

On January 17, 1994, exactly one year before the Great Hanshin-Awaji Earthquake, a magnitude 6.8 earthquake struck California. In the so-called Northridge Earthquake, 57 people died and 7,300 people were injured. The major expressways were heavily damaged. While the population and housing density are different from those in Japan, the level of damage was much smaller compared to the Great Hanshin-Awaji Earthquake centered in Kobe.

In 1986, one year after a magnitude 8.0 Mexico City earthquake killed more than ten thousand, California passed the California Earthquake Hazards Reduction Act. That act is said to be the most advanced earthquake and disaster management law in the world, as its construction standards, level of people's awareness of earthquakes, and sharing of information are all very high. When a home is sold, for example, the seller is obligated to provide information on the possible damage that would be incurred in an earthquake.

In late 2005 a scandal rocked Japan that had to do with an architect's having designed buildings that did not meet earthquake resistance standards, allegedly due to pressure by a construction company to reduce costs. Based on blueprints using falsified data, condominiums and hotels were built that were not reinforced and were likely to collapse in the event of an earthquake of magnitude 5 or greater. For example, the use of steel supports was greatly reduced. The news often used the word "life-threatening," and indeed these examples of intentionally falsifying data and not using proper construction techniques and materials were very much serious criminal acts that threatened the lives of the people living in and using those buildings. Moreover, this scandal exposed problems in the inspection system, which was supposed to check on the designs used to construct the buildings. An immediate review of this system is necessary.

Yokohama City and Los Angeles established the Yokohama–Los Angeles Disaster Prevention Policy Conference, holding its first meeting in November 2001. Yokohama is introducing a system called READY, which is a real-time disaster preparation system based on the CUBE system mentioned above. This system is based on the premise that after an earthquake, it will be difficult to get information from the affected areas, and thus it estimates the damage and simulates a response plan ahead of time. It is comprised of the following:

1. A High-Density, Strong-Motion Seismograph Network (Kō-mitsudo Kyōshinkei Netowaaku). Within three minutes of an earthquake, seismic information is gathered from 150 sensors set two kilometers apart from each other throughout the city. This information is transferred to three other locations, including the disaster response headquarters.

2. A Seismic Damage Estimate Geographic Information System (Shindo Higai Suitei Chiri Jōhō Shisutemu). Within ten minutes of an earthquake and with the data gathered, estimates are provided about the possibility of landslides and liquefaction, as well as the number of collapsed wooden houses and which areas are damaged. At the same time, the system identifies safe roads to use for emergency and other relief-related transport, evacuation shelters, and hospitals.

3. Intranet GIS (Higai Jōhō Shūshū-Shūyaku Shisutemu). Sixty minutes after an earthquake, information on damage to roadways and homes is collected at the disaster response offices.

This system has the merit of being able to prepare an effective response even before enough information is gathered because the initial data are collected immediately following an earthquake. There was a lack of information for a long time following the Great Hanshin-Awaji Earthquake, making it difficult to know what response to undertake.

In Yokoyama City there is a disaster-monitoring camera (*saigai kanshi kamera*) set up in the 296-meter-high Landmark Tower, from which some 70 percent of the city can be seen. Moreover, an imagery relaying system with cameras is being installed in helicopters so that they can fly over disaster areas and relay live video images to related organizations and officials. The central government is also developing this system.

The DIS of the Ministry of Land, Infrastructure, and Transport is meant to help with a rapid response to emergency repairs through the early gathering of disaster information and its sharing with related organizations. Specifically combining data from all around the country about topography, foundations, architecture, and population, with earthquake information provided from the Metrological Agency, this system can estimate seismic activity, building damage, and the human toll. The DIS turns on automatically following an earthquake with an intensity of 4 on the seismic scale, and within thirty minutes it can complete the aforementioned estimates.

In addition, the Emergency Measures System (Ōkyū Taisaku Shien Shisutemu) seeks to provide effective responses in a disaster by combining information input on roadways, rail lines, other transportation networks, fire stations, hospitals, and other disaster-related centers with maps of disaster-affected areas. Moreover, the Recovery and Reconstruction System, or RRS (Fukkyū to Fukkō Shien Shisutemu) goes into effect approximately one week after a disaster.

These kinds of systems, which are meant to assess the situation quickly following a disaster (when information is limited and scattered) and develop a quick response, are spreading from prefectures and cities to the private sector. Tokyo Gas's SIGNAL (Jishin Jidō Kankō Keihō Shisutemu), Kawasaki City's Earthquake Response Support System (Shinsai Taisaku Shien Shisutemu), and the Tokyo Metropolitan Fire Department's Disaster Early Estimates System (Sōki Higai Suitei Shisutemu) are such examples.

Create a Japanese Version of FEMA

Readers may remember the so-called Hyper-Rescue Force (Haipaa Resukyūtai) that served at the time of the Niigata-Chuetsu Earthquake in October 2004. It was particularly involved in trying to help one family that was buried alive in a vehicle in a landslide. Using the latest technology and skills, the force was able to rescue a child from the vehicle.

The real name of the force is the Fire Rescue Task Force (Shōbō Kyūjō Kidō Butai). The task force has units established within several existing fire district headquarters of the Tokyo Fire Department (Tōkyō Shōbōchō): at the Second Fire District Headquarters, which covers the districts of Shinagawa, Oi, Ebara, Omori, Daen Chofu, Urata, and Yaguchi; at the Third Fire District Headquarters, which covers the districts of Meguro, Setaya, Tamagawa, Seijo, and Shibuya; and at the Eighth Fire District Headquarters, which covers the cities of Tachikawa, Musashino, and Miitake, among other areas. The task force teams are made up of personnel who have special knowledge and skills relating to large-scale disasters and large emergency vehicles. The teams can also respond to fires in warehouses and factories, underground subways and malls, and chemical factories, among other large-scale disasters. The Third Fire District team includes personnel especially trained in handling nuclear, biological, and chemical disasters and possesses a high degree of expertise and the special equipment and vehicles to deal with such disasters.

In addition, the Fire Rescue Task Force has vehicles equipped with cranes and winches, illumination equipment, and generators, among other things. It also has emergency vehicles that can get into disaster areas on roads that otherwise might be impassible. In addition to having rescue equipment found in other emergency service units, it also has special search and rescue equipment that uses magnetic and sonar technologies.

The Fire Rescue Task Force, often called by its nickname, the Hyper-Rescue Force, was established in 1995 based on some of the lessons of the Great Hanshin-Awaji Earthquake and is intended to make rescue operations faster and more effective. In the event of a large-scale natural disaster, the director general of the Fire and Disaster Management Agency can dispatch the Fire Rescue Task Force, comprising expert firefighters gathered from all over the country, to undertake rescue operations over a wide area.

Members of the Fire Rescue Task Force are chosen from 777 fire departments out of a total of 894 nationwide. Those selected are then asked to register to be on call as part of the Fire Rescue Task Force. Ten years after its founding, there were more than thirty-one thousand firefighters registered from 2,210 fire stations around the country.

Each task force has a Command Response Team, Rescue Team, Emergency Team, Firefighting Team, Logistical Support Team, Air Squadron, Marine Squadron, Special Disaster Team, and Special Equipment Team. The Command Response Team can be deployed quickly to a disaster area using helicopters and other means to assess the disaster situation; it can then contact and liaison with the Fire and Disaster Management Agency and provide instructions and support to local firefighting teams. The Special Disaster Teams, moreover, can respond to special disaster situations, such as petroleum and chemical fires, poisonous and toxic substance spills, and nuclear radiation accidents.

With the revision of the Fire and Disaster Management Organization Law (Shōbō Soshikihō) in June 2003, the director general of the Fire and Disaster Management Agency can now order the dispatch of the task force in large-scale disasters that involve two or more prefectures or if a nuclear-biological-chemical (NBC) disaster situation arises. At the same time financial support would be provided for the improvement of fire departments and other facilities based on the Basic Plan of the Fire Rescue Task Force (Kinkyū Shōbō Kyūentai Kihon Keikaku) in such cases. In other words, all fire departments throughout the country are required to respond to a major disaster by sending forces, the expenses to be covered by the national government. Incidentally, in the first fiscal year after the Basic Plan was issued, 4.8 billion yen ($48 million) was spent by the central government for such deployments. The task force was deployed to the Northern Miyagi Prefecture Earthquake (Miyagiken Hokubu Jishin) in late July 2003, a fire at the Tochigi Plant of the Bridgestone Tire Company in early September 2003, and the Tokatsu Earthquake (Tokatsuoki Jishin) later that same month.

The following is a description of the mission behind the establishment of FEMA in 1979: "FEMA's mission is to support our citizens and first responders to ensure that as a nation we work together to build, sustain, and improve our capability to prepare for, protect against, respond to, recover from, and mitigate all hazards."[16]

FEMA is in charge of the immediate response to disasters that strike. In addition to streamlining information about disasters, it is, as was explained above, an independent government agency involved in crisis management that is directly under the president and that is comprised of experts on disasters, including those on terrorism and poison gas. It is in charge of various government organizations involved in emergency responses, such as the Emergency Broadcasting System and federal disaster relief organizations. Its main responsibilities are to oversee the relief and recovery operations at a time of disaster, prepare disaster response plans, provide financial support to state and local governments for disaster preparedness, manage government financial assistance in times of disaster, and handle the flow of recovery funds.

In the past, preparation for natural disasters was considered a type of "insurance" against disasters. However, FEMA sees that disasters are repeating events. Some are large, some are small, but regardless of the scale, disasters will occur. As such, FEMA believes it is important to plan, prepare, and constantly reexamine the systems in place to make them more efficient. In other words, disasters will recur, and FEMA considers the money used for preparing for disasters as a wise and necessary expense. FEMA sees disaster response as a life cycle and believes it is important to develop the disaster response capabilities step by step along the following lines.

1. Reduce the risk of emergencies and disasters. Based on the information on disasters to date, review, plan, and prepare the necessary legislation and building codes and ensure the mitigation of future disasters.
2. Mitigate the effects of emergencies and disasters. Each public organization and related organizations prepare detailed disaster response plans and manuals based on the laws and plans created in the earlier phase.

3. Prepare for emergencies and disasters. Improve disaster drills, storage capabilities, and other facilities in order to be able to withstand a disaster.

4. Respond to emergencies and disasters. Undertake immediate search-and-rescue and firefighting operations at the time of a disaster in order to limit the extent of damage.

5. Recover from emergencies and disasters. For several months to several years after a disaster hits, not only help restore electricity, water, gas, and other public services; provide temporary housing; and repair infrastructure, but also help victims of the disaster get back on their feet financially.

6. Rebuild for the future. In this phase bridges and buildings are constructed so as to be safe from the dangers of earthquakes, flooding, and other disasters, taking into account new building standards, which should be updated as necessary so that structures can withstand earthquakes and typhoons, thereby reducing the damage as much as possible.

FEMA is concerned about various types of disasters, from natural disasters to large-scale disasters at public and other facilities to man-made disasters. Natural disasters include earthquakes, heat waves, flooding, hurricanes, typhoons, tornados, tsunamis, volcanic eruptions, wildfires, blizzards, cold fronts, lightning, and landslides, among other things. Disasters at public facilities include electricity blackouts and problems, gas explosions, gas leaks, problems at chemical plants, radiation problems, fires at residential and commercial properties, and disasters at nuclear power plants. FEMA also responds to criminal activities, including terrorism.

When such large-scale disasters occur, FEMA, which is headed by a presidentially appointed director who serves as the highest in command, organizes all of the national and state agencies and Red Cross, all of which are placed under FEMA's control. In particular FEMA makes an effort to create a structure to gather information in times of crisis.

However, there were problems with FEMA's response at the time of the hugely destructive Hurricane Katrina, which struck the Gulf

Coast of the United States in late August 2005. Katrina recorded wind speeds of seventy-eight meters per second and was designated a category 5, the highest on the scale of hurricane measurements. Hurricane Katrina ended up killing more than one thousand people. In particular when the levees broke, the Mississippi River overflowed and flooded New Orleans. FEMA did not function well and ended up making many things worse.

Different reasons are given for FEMA's failures then. One is that Katrina management was placed under the Department of Homeland Security, set up as a result of the September 11, 2001, terrorist attacks, and thus the problem became larger and more bureaucratic. Another explanation is that the director and senior leadership were incompetent political appointees with no practical experience with disasters. Other reasons are given too, but in any case the slow and inappropriate response to the disaster was mainly due to the reorganization of FEMA under the Department of Homeland Security and the poor quality of the senior leadership. A reexamination of the way FEMA did business was begun after the Katrina catastrophe.

There are two approaches in research with regard to earthquakes. One concerns the study of earthquakes themselves, including the ability to predict them. The other accepts the fact that earthquakes occur and focuses on disaster management and mitigation, an area that has been getting increasing attention.

In the Sumatra earthquake as well, if the residents had had a better awareness and understanding of tsunamis, the number of those lost would likely have been a fraction of the real figure of more than 220,000. If the tide recedes from the coast in an unusual way, it could mean that a tsunami is coming. In addition, even if the first wave comes and goes, a second or third wave might be on its way. Furthermore, the second wave will likely ride the first wave, becoming bigger. A person fleeing from a tsunami must get to high ground and not stop even if that person thinks he or she is far enough away. If those fleeing had known they had to be on higher ground, more could have been saved.

Preparing for Future Earthquakes

As noted above, earthquake research in Japan has evolved a great deal since the passage of the Large-Scale Earthquake Countermeasures Law in 1978. There has been a lot of investment in facilities to predict a Tokai earthquake, but no dramatic results have appeared to date. While it is important to continue with research and observations to predict earthquakes, it is also important to understand that research on the mechanisms of earthquakes may also lead to the ability to predict them.

At the same time it is becoming more necessary to think about disaster management and disaster mitigation. Even if it becomes possible to predict earthquakes in the future, it will not be possible to reduce the size of the earthquake or control it in any way. As a result, it will be important to construct buildings, towns, roads, railways, etc. that can withstand an earthquake.

In January 2005, three weeks after the Sumatra earthquake and Indian Ocean tsunami, the United Nations sponsored a World Conference on Disaster Reduction that was held in Kobe. There officials, scholars, and experts discussed how mankind could stand up to the ravages of nature. Among the discussions was a proposal for the creation of a worldwide tsunami early-warning system. In addition, disaster preparedness and disaster mitigation were also discussed.

Japan is a "natural disaster superpower" in the sense that it faces an abnormally large amount of natural disasters. Although it possesses less than 0.25 percent of the earth's land mass, more than 10 percent of the large earthquakes and volcanic eruptions have occurred here. Japan sits atop four tectonic plates and is along the path of many of the typhoons that emerge near the equator. In addition to the damage from typhoons that occur each year, the people of Japan have to live with preparing for tsunamis as well.

Among the organizations helping to prepare for a disaster is the Central Disaster Management Council. There is even a minister in charge of disaster management whose existence is not really considered in ordinary times. Many institutes, committees, and centers devoted to earthquake research have sprung up, like bamboo after a rain. Even the Headquarters for Earthquake Research Promotion is run by officials sent from several ministries and agencies. The existence of these similar organizations leaves one to believe that rather than striving for efficiency, these different ministries and agencies are simply competing with one another for influence and budget allocations.

Because of the destructive typhoons that come to Japan every year and the likelihood of a major disaster, such as an earthquake or volcanic eruption, it is important that the politicians, bureaucrats, and academics end their power struggles and instead focus on establishing one authoritative organization that will be able to respond to such disasters in an effective manner. This organization does not have to be like FEMA in the United States (which, as noted, also deals with terrorist attacks and nuclear power plant accidents) but should instead focus on natural disasters. It can be a comprehensive organization that would conduct scientific research on typhoons, flooding, earthquakes, and volcanic eruptions; prepare for disasters; and mitigate against them. Its bureaucratic level should be high, and it can even be made an "agency" within the national government. The Central Disaster Management Council and the Headquarters for Earthquake Research Promotion should be combined to create this organization, and other institutes and committees could be merged within it. It could be named the Natural Disaster Research and Response Agency (Shizen Saigai Kenkyū Taisakuchō). It could have a supervisory division, a measures (or response) division, and a research division.

The supervisory division would be something akin to a merger of the Central Disaster Management Council and the Policy Committee of the Headquarters for Earthquake Research Promotion. It would be responsible for deciding the national approach to dealing with future natural disasters. The measures (or response) division would pursue research on disaster management and mitigation and conduct training in these areas. For example, it would prepare damage estimates, basic hazard maps, and more detailed maps after visiting and consulting with local authorities and experts. Furthermore, in an actual disaster situation it would be in charge of all other organizations. Moreover, it would create a manual for recovery and reconstruction following a large-scale disaster and serve as an organizer for those efforts.

The research division would oversee research on typhoons, earthquakes, volcanic eruptions, etc. It would unify the various basic research that is being conducting in an uncoordinated manner with research about disaster preparedness and management and create a more efficient research environment.

The damage caused by the Great Hanshin-Awaji Earthquake was estimated at 13 trillion yen ($130 billion) and that of the Niigata-Chuetsu Earthquake was more than 470 billion yen ($4.7 billion). The damaged incurred every year in typhoons and heavy rains amounts to billions and sometimes tens of billions of yen. If this new organization is set up and is able to reduce the damage by one-third or more through disaster mitigation, it will have performed a very valuable role. It would be especially good if this organization could share with other countries Japan's knowledge of and experiences with disasters.

Conclusion

No one will forget the year 2004. Several typhoons, one after the other, struck Japan, and there was heavy rain and unprecedented flooding around the country. In addition, the magnitude 7 Niigata-Chuetsu Earthquake occurred, causing, for the first time since it had opened, the derailing of a Shinkansen line. And, of course, there was the Sumatra earthquake and tsunami, which was one of the worst disasters in history. It goes without saying, however, that as long as we live on this planet, we have to deal with all that it has to offer, including disasters. We cannot control nature, and we have to disabuse ourselves of the idea that we can. We live amid nature, not above it, and thus we have to learn about it and learn how to live on this planet.

The Japanese government's response to the October 2004 Niigata-Chuetsu Earthquake was fairly quick. In particular the responses of the SDF and Fire and Disaster Management Agency were quite fast. The bridges and overpasses of the bullet train line and expressways held up and did not collapse. It can be said that the lessons of the earthquake nine years before in southern Hyogo were utilized to develop concrete measures. However, private homes collapsed, mountainsides crumbled, and tunnels and roadways between mountains were destroyed. It is a fact, therefore, that some private homeowners did little to prepare their homes for earthquakes, and earthquake preparations at the local level were similarly inadequate.

After a disaster happens, all we can do is simply to react. What is important, however, is the preparation beforehand. In this sense both the government and the people were ill-prepared.

The Central Disaster Management Council has announced its estimates in the event that Tokai, Tonankai, and Nankai earthquakes occurred simultaneously. Using the assumption that a magnitude 8.7 earthquake hits, the council predicts in a worst-case situation that there would be twenty-eight thousand dead and that the economic damage, both direct and indirect, would amount to 81 trillion yen ($0.8 trillion). [After the March 11 disaster the estimates for the number of dead were multiplied by twelve and the economic damage by five.] If even 10 percent of this sum of money were used for disaster preparedness, the economic impact of such a disaster would be reduced to half or even one-tenth, and the future impact of an economic recession (or depression) nationally or worldwide would be decreased.

In addition, on November 17, 2004, the Earthquake Working Group of the Central Disaster Prevention Council's Tokyo Earthquake Countermeasures Experts Committee (Shuto Chokka Jishin Taisaku Senmon Chōsakai) published a map with the likely seismic intensity points in the event of an earthquake occurring directly under the capital area in Tokyo. It shows that throughout a wide area of the capital there will be shaking in the order of 6-weak on the seismic Richter scale, while in some areas it will be a stronger or even more violent 7. In December the Working Group examined the impact on human life and buildings, but the results of the study did not realistically reflect the scale of the damage. I beg those who are involved in preparing disaster plans to make accurate assessments because so many lives are at stake.

Regardless of whether it is possible or not to predict earthquakes, earthquake prediction is still sort of a reactive approach to disasters. If we knew an earthquake was to strike tomorrow, at best we might think about gathering up our belongings and heading to an emergency evacuation shelter. From there we would only be able to stand and watch houses collapse and mountains fall until the earthquake and its aftershocks subsided.

For future earthquakes it is necessary not only to continue basic research on earthquakes themselves, as well as steady research on earthquake prediction, but to even more proactively undertake disaster prevention and mitigation. Buildings should be constructed that can withstand earthquakes. The same is true for tunnels, expressways, subways, and towns. The goal of government and the mindset of the people should be the same—that is, even if a disaster occurs, the destruction must be limited to the greatest extent possible.

At the same time it is probably necessary for a country like Japan, which is faced with many natural disasters, to have a national level "agency" to promote disaster preparedness and mitigation. In addition to the direct-hit-on-Tokyo scenario, there are the trench-type earthquakes that would likely cause a tsunami. These potential disasters should not be handled in a haphazard manner after the fact but need to be prepared for ahead of time.

It is a fact that strain energy is being built up underneath Japan and that something will set this energy loose, triggering an earthquake. We may not know when it will come, but it is certain that it will come. If there is still a great deal of damage and destruction following an earthquake that we knew was coming and knew to expect, it will be not only a natural disaster, but a human catastrophe on top of that.

As long as we live in this country, so full of earthquakes, we citizens must be able to respond to earthquakes on our own and not rely exclusively on the government.[1]

Epilogue

TAKASHIMA TETSUO WITH ROBERT D. ELDRIDGE

Friday afternoon, March 11, 2011.

As I always do, I went to the gym, did some shopping, and returned home and turned on the television. My eyes became glued to the TV. The tsunami was flowing over the embankments, devouring everything in its path, including buildings, cars, boats, and people. Greenhouses were being pushed along from the coast deep inland. The images I had described in my book *Tsunami* were playing out on television.[1] I changed channels, but still it was the same live video feeds from the Tohoku region. The tragedy that was affecting northeast Japan was being shown frighteningly, in real time, before my eyes.

Images of the constant, never-ending destruction and moving debris were repeated on TV all day the following day. They showed communities where homes had stood, where families had lived, and where people had worked. Now, however, there were no signs that life had existed there at all. The tsunami had swallowed up people, destroyed towns, and washed away the past, the present, and the future.

This was the Great East Japan Earthquake and Tsunami, which took the lives of almost twenty thousand people, including those still missing.

Immediately after this disaster, helping hands were extended to northeast Japan from all over the world. In particular the support of the U.S. military in Operation Tomodachi (Tomodachi Sakusen) gave much hope and comfort not only to the victims of the disaster area, but also to all the people of Japan.

The world is indeed interconnected. We are not alone. I have never felt these words to be so true as I do now.

Currently the planet is facing a huge problem with global warming. The massive typhoons, flooding, destructive rains, and overall unusual weather that we have seen so frequently in recent years are attributed to this global warming.

When a large-scale disaster occurs, it does not matter where or when, as disaster is similar around the world. People in underground malls, subways, tunnels, and other enclosed areas will panic. There will be a danger of fires and flooding. People traveling on high-speed trains and expressways will be frightened.

Under the earth there are a lot of tectonic plates that are overlapping and moving. The energy being built up by this friction is growing, and when it has reached a critical point, it will have to snap. This is an earthquake.

Large-scale earthquakes happen in every part of the world. A certain degree of awareness and level of preparation may be the difference between life and death. While it is impossible to prevent an earthquake, there is a long list of things that can be done ahead of time. In particular *knowledge* is the most important aspect of disaster preparedness and mitigation.

I would be very happy if this book, now available in English, were to contribute to this knowledge and assist you in your understanding of the dangers that earthquakes and tsunamis in particular present, based on our experiences in Japan. Please note that the book was originally written in 2006 and that many of the assumptions that have gone into disaster planning are being reconsidered and much information is being updated now (some of which has been included in the footnotes or in this epilogue). However, many problems and issues identified here will continue to affect us now and in the future. Indeed, if anything, the estimates for the amount of destruction are many, many times worse. The challenge now, as it has been in the past, is to improve upon the ability to predict, prepare, mitigate, and respond, as well as to make sure lessons are shared and passed down to future generations. "Expect the unexpected," one newspaper editorial entreated us in early 2012 on the seventeenth anniversary of the Great Hanshin-Awaji Earthquake.[2] Expect another disaster, another complex disaster, to happen again and again.

I would like to express my deep gratitude to Dr. Robert D. Eldridge, who was a key figure in Operation Tomodachi as the political adviser to the Forward Command Element of United States Forces Japan, working out of Camp Sendai in Miyagi Prefecture, for his assistance with translating and annotating the original version of this book and providing additional help with this epilogue for the English version.

Although much has been learned and tested as a result of the March 11, 2011, Great East Japan Earthquake and Tsunami (not to mention nuclear disaster), many of the warnings and concerns introduced in this book, written years before that triple disaster, still apply today. This epilogue will introduce some significant updates to Japan's preparedness and disaster management system in the wake of "3/11."

While many of the efforts have been admirable in that the various findings and recommendations have become more realistic, I (and Dr. Eldridge from an American, albeit personal, perspective) would argue there is still much more to be done, such as furthering the pace and quality of national disaster planning up and down the chain as well as laterally and, equally important, integrating U.S. forces in Japan into some of the planning for the responses *ahead of time*.[3]

The most important advancement is the fact that Japan's estimates have become more convincing. Throughout the original book I warned—as has the translator warned in his foreword— that estimates used by the central government and local governments (such as Tokyo) have been extremely unrealistic, almost criminally so. With more accurate numbers it is hoped that planners will find better ways to mitigate problems, that organizations that need to work together will more rapidly develop realistic responses, and that residents will take extra precautions. So often in the immediate days following the March 11 tragedy, we heard that the scale of the earthquake, tsunami, and nuclear meltdown was "beyond expectations" (*sōteigai*) Let us work to make sure that this is not the case following the next natural or man-made disaster.

A good start in this direction was made when the Cabinet Office established, albeit somewhat belatedly, the sixteen-member Study Group on a Megaquake in the Nankai Trough (Nankai Trafu no Kyodai Jishin Moderu Kentōkai) in late August 2011.[4] In March 2012 the Study Group prepared its first report on likely seismic intensity and trouble spots, including tsunami heights.[5] By August its second report came out—estimating that as many as 151 cities, towns, and villages in more than ten prefectures would experience the highest levels of shaking on the Japanese seismic scale (7), Kochi Prefecture would be inundated with tsunamis as high as thirty-four meters, and as many as 323,000 might die as a result of a megaquake along the Nankai Trough.[6] Shizuoka Prefecture is believed likely to be the hardest hit, with 109,000 dead.

Sadly the findings of the Study Group are not available in English, with the exception of the occasional story in the newspapers. This problem—the lack of readily available, yet specialized, information in English about Japan—remains a serious concern, as it was prior to March 11. The government of Japan is getting better at this, but the record remains spotty. Sharing such information through regular briefings with the embassies of the various countries in Japan's capital is vital for both the safety and welfare of foreign nationals, as well as to help those countries plan how best to come to Japan's aid if requested.

Of course some experts challenge the idea that accurate predictions are possible or to what degree they are possible. This remains an issue of heated discussion in some circles. Robert Geller, a professor of seismology at Tokyo University, is adamant that earthquakes cannot currently be accurately predicted, and he published *Nihonjin ha shiranai "jishin yochi" no seitai* (What Japanese do not know about the actual state of "earthquake prediction") in the summer of 2011.[7] Others, such as Hayakawa Masashi, a professor emeritus of the University of Electro-Communications (Denki Tsūshin Daigaku), insists prediction is possible, publishing a book in December 2011 entitled *Jishin ga yochi dekiru!* (Earthquakes can be predicted!).[8] "I have no intention," Hayakawa explained to a reporter, "of arguing with any doubters. Prediction is possible, we have proven that, and until I can convince the government that this kind of research is essential for public safety, I will have to find ways of funding it myself."[9]

As the above studies and debates were taking place, another body, the Committee for Policy Planning for Disaster Management (Bōsai Taisaku Suishin Kentō Iinkai), was established under the Central Disaster Management Council on October 11, 2011, seven months to the day after the March 11 disaster. After thirteen meetings, on July 12, 2012, the committee released its report, which is fortunately available in English.[10]

As the committee's report was being generated, the Working Group on Measures to Respond to a Megaquake in the Nankai Trough (Nankai Torafu Kyodai Jishin Taisaku Kentō Waaking Guruupu) was established on March 7, 2012, to prepare estimates of the human, material, and economic damage likely in such a disaster, based on the lessons learned from the March 11 tragedy. The Working Group conducted its first meeting on April 20 and completed its report a year later on May 28, 2013.[11]

While the renewed interest in disaster management is praiseworthy and more refined research and conclusions are admirable in the wake of the March 11 disaster, the proliferation of study groups is indeed confusing and may lead to bureaucratic solutions (or non-solutions) to unconventional and "unexpected" problems. I warned of this in the original book, arguing that much time, money, and effort were being wasted with such a proliferation of groups and organizations.

One committee not previously introduced is the Council on Measures to Respond to a Megaquake in the Nankai Trough (Nankai Torafu Kyodai Jishin Taisaku Kyōgikai), which appears to have been established 2012 for the purpose of coordinating among different organizations in both the public and private sectors before, during, and after a crisis.[12] Its first meeting was held in June in Osaka, attended by 169 people from 136 different entities, and the second in early August at the Tokyo Rinkai Disaster Prevention Park (Tōkyō Rinkai Kōiki Bōsai Kōen), attended by 174 people from 119 organizations. It appears the council has not officially met since then but has instead facilitated the creation of regional blocs that meet on their own. One such gathering is the Kyushu Bloc, established on

August 30, 2012. Several other blocs have been created as well. However, the frequency of the meetings of the various blocs varies, as does the perception of the dangers among the various organizations and entities.

Because of such differences, some localities are moving forward on their own, setting their own pace. Shizuoka Prefecture, under the dynamic leadership of Governor Kawakatsu Keita, is truly speeding ahead, forging prefectural, national, local, and even bilateral cooperation; integrating U.S. forces into the prefecture's disaster drills; and establishing personnel exchanges with the U.S. Marine Corps. Kawakatsu's leadership has identified gaps in national planning and coordination, and the prefecture is helping to fill them on its own. While not perfect, Shizuoka's preparations and outlook, as well as the degree of cooperation it has established with U.S. personnel, are a model for the rest of Japan.

In the meantime, the Japan Meteorological Agency has announced, effective August 30, 2013, that it will launch an emergency warning system that improves on the warnings for tsunamis, flooding, and volcanoes. It is important that the JMA created an English website on June 21, 2013, and is uploading an increasing amount of information on it. There is still much more to do, but its efforts can be applauded.

One expert and prolific writer on crisis management, Yanagida Kunio, who was very critical of the way the Central Disaster Management Council had handled things prior to the March 11 disaster—namely, its unwillingness to entertain theories that suggested a greater tsunami height and thus more extensive damage—praised the fact that the Committee for Technical Investigation on Countermeasures for Earthquakes and Tsunamis Based on the Lessons Learned from the "2011 Off the Pacific Coast of Tohoku Earthquake" (Tōhoku Chihō Taiheiyō Oki Jishin o Kyōkun to Shita Jishin-Tsunami Taisaku ni Kansuru Senmon Chōsakai), which was established on April 27, 2011, "completely reversed its previous way of thinking compared to before the earthquake by 180 degrees."[13] The writer meant that the committee was willing to consider more possible scenarios, even if the degree of certainty was unclear. In other words, it was trying to "think outside the box." In addition, the committee promoted transparency and aggressively released its findings, even publishing the final report, submitted on September 28, 2011, in English.[14]

One of the members of the committee, Tokyo University professor emeritus Shimazaki Kunihiko, described in an interview how the pre-3/11 discussions tended to be based on groupthink:

> It was truly regrettable. We had all the "brains" in the country focused on earthquake studies assembled in the group. Nevertheless, our report was rejected. I should have pursued it more, but it got to the point that no matter what I said, it was not listened to. The Central Disaster Management Council is in charge of all earthquake measures, and I could not fight it single-handedly. I felt a sense of despair not to be able to overturn its decision. I am still traumatized by the experience.[15]

Because of these factors, one observer echoed the feelings of many people when he said that it was "vital that experts regain the trust of the public."[16] The same can be said of Japan's political leaders and bureaucracy, a view held by those both inside and outside of Japan. The country is in its third administration since the March 2011 disaster.[17] One wonders if the politics of malaise, as witnessed over the previous two decades, or if a renewed, united effort to truly bring about Japan's renaissance will prevail.[18] Fortunately there is hope.

In addition to the revisions of the disaster estimates that are facilitating improvements to disaster preparedness efforts throughout the country, another effort in the wake of 3/11 has been a flexible and more thoughtful approach to recovery through the establishment of the Great East Japan Earthquake Reconstruction Design Council (Higashi Nihon Daishinsai Fukkō Kōsō Kaigi), headed by Dr. Iokibe Makoto, an award-winning scholar and president of the National Defense Academy (NDA) at the time of the earthquake. Although there was some criticism that Prime Minister Kan Naoto had appointed "a political historian" to chair the council, in fact Iokibe, who was previously a professor at Kobe University and had lost his home in the Great Hanshin-Awaji Earthquake, had been heavily involved in the recovery efforts after 1995, including conducting candid assessments of the response based on unprecedented access to decision makers and officials.[19] In addition, as a historian of modern Japan and a specialist on the Allied Occupation of Japan, Iokibe was able to compare the recovery efforts following the 1923 Great Kanto Earthquake, the destruction in Japan at the end of World War II, the Kobe earthquake, and the Tohoku disaster, focusing on fiscal policies, political decisions, examples of determined leadership, and the shaping of public opinion. Indeed as the former supervisor of Lieutenant General Kimizuka Eiji, the commander of the Joint Task Force–Tohoku (Tōgō Ninmu Butai–TH), who had previously served under Iokibe as deputy commandant of the NDA, and as the former academic adviser of Eldridge, who was serving as the political adviser to the Forward Command Element of U.S. Forces in Sendai, Iokibe was well versed on what was going on up north shortly after the disaster happened and the response was forming.

The council was created a month after the disaster on April 11 by Cabinet decision. It comprised sixteen members, under which sat nineteen experts and some fifty officials from a cross-section of government agencies, and it included the governors of the most affected prefectures. It met twelve times over the course of seventy-five days and included, according to Iokibe, meetings that were quite "heated" and would last six hours.[20] Iokibe praised the cooperation that was found among the government agencies, which usually work independently in a stovepiped manner or in some cases at cross-purposes.

Upon its formation, Iokibe and the members of the council went to Tohoku to begin their investigations. He later recalled:

As I live in Kobe, Hyogo Prefecture, my house was damaged during the Great Hanshin-Awaji Earthquake of 1995, due to subsidence caused by cracks in the ground. Some of the traditional Japanese-style wooden houses in my neighborhood were completely destroyed. In that sense, the damage caused by the Great Hanshin-Awaji Earthquake was fairly selective, even within the same area. This time, however, the tsunami that followed the Great East Japan Earthquake laid waste to more or less everything in its way. I went to see some of the affected areas along the Pacific coast in Tohoku a month after the quake, and the entire town had been reduced to rubble. Even the hospital, the town hall, and other steel-reinforced public buildings that had been designed to withstand disasters had been devastated. Looking out at that deserted landscape was a real shock. It seemed almost unreal.[21]

The council's recommendations were submitted on June 25. On that occasion Iokibe explained at a press conference some of the basic ideas behind the recommendations:

Clearly we know now that it is impossible to physically defend our towns against a tsunami of that scale. The reconstruction process will therefore need to focus on the concept of "disaster reduction," aimed at minimizing damage utilizing various means in the event of a natural disaster rather than preventing it entirely. With that in mind, our report has proposed the mass relocation of coastal towns and villages in the affected area to higher ground, although facilities for fisheries should be rebuilt near the coast. We have proposed creating entirely new communities on the hill, including facilities such as schools, hospitals, and care homes, as well as residential properties, creating a fully integrated local care structure to cope with the aged society.[22]

At the press conference Iokibe noted that the council was grateful for the international support Japan received following the disaster, and the council wanted to reciprocate by submitting a report that was transparent, accessible, and inclusive. The report, available in English, is entitled "Toward Reconstruction: Hope Beyond the Disaster" (Fukkō e no teigen: Hisan no naka no kibō) and is comprised of a prologue, epilogue, and four chapters.[23]

The report was written in part by Mikuriya Takashi, then with the Research Center for Advanced Science and Technology at Tokyo University (Tōkyō Daigaku Sentan Kagaku Gijutsu Kenkyū Sentaa), and Iio Jun of the National Graduate Institute for Policy Studies (Seisaku Kenkyū Daigakuin Daigaku). Both Mikuriya and Iio emphasized seven principles to which the council members would constantly return when the discussions became unwieldy:

Seven Principles for the Reconstruction Framework

Principle 1: For us, the survivors, there is no other starting point for the path to recovery than to remember and honor the many lives that have been lost. Accordingly we shall record the disaster for eternity, including through the creation of memorial forests and monuments, and we shall have the disaster scientifically analyzed by a broad range of scholars to draw lessons that will be shared with the world and passed down to posterity.

Principle 2: Given the vastness and diversity of the disaster region, we shall make community-focused reconstruction the foundation of efforts toward recovery. The national government will support that reconstruction through general guidelines and institutional design.

Principle 3: In order to revive disaster-afflicted Tohoku, we shall pursue forms of recovery and reconstruction that tap into the region's latent strengths and lead to technological innovation. We shall strive to develop this region's socioeconomic potential to lead Japan in the future.

Principle 4: While preserving the strong bonds of local residents, we shall construct disaster-resilient safe and secure communities and natural energy-powered region.

Principle 5: Japan's economy cannot be restored unless the disaster areas are rebuilt. The disaster areas cannot be truly rebuilt unless Japan's economy is restored. Recognizing these facts, we shall simultaneously pursue reconstruction of the afflicted areas and revitalization of the nation.

Principle 6: We shall seek an early resolution of the nuclear accidents and shall devote closer attention to support and recovery efforts for the areas affected by the accidents.

Principle 7: All of us living now shall view the disaster as affecting our own lives and shall pursue reconstruction with a spirit of solidarity and mutual understanding that permeates the entire nation.

At the press conference Iokibe stressed that the task ahead was going to be difficult, but Japanese history was literally one of natural calamities, and the country had rebounded before every time. Because of this expectation of a rebound, Iokibe was frustrated later that year with the slow pace of the government's and Diet's actions on the council's recommendations, and he publicly criticized the government.[24] The famous writer Funabashi Yoichi warned the government (and country as a whole) around this time that "The choice is rebirth or ruin."[25] Eventually a bipartisan effort was made and funds were approved to begin implementing the council's recommendations. Prime Minister Noda Yoshihiko subsequently announced in a *Washington Post* op-ed that the Japanese government was indeed committed to rebuilding.[26]

On February 10, 2012, the council's work officially came to an end with the establishment of the Reconstruction Agency (Fukkōchō).[27] The new agency is meant to coordinate across ministries and agencies to assist communities affected by the earthquake, tsunami, and nuclear disaster. Iokibe now serves as the chairman of an advisory committee for the new agency called the Reconstruction Promotion Committee (Fukkō Suishin Iinkai), which has met officially a half-dozen times, as well as undertaking an equal number of investigative trips to the disaster region.

On the second anniversary of the disaster Iokibe published an article about the state of the recovery efforts and the work of the council and the committee that followed it. He described the reconstruction of the Tohoku region as a chance to revitalize all of Japan and to get it out of its twenty-year malaise, known as the "Lost Two Decades."[28]

One extremely problematic issue that will complicate reconstruction and that has truly made the disaster a complex one is that of the Fukushima Daiichi Nuclear Power Plant. First, there are the environmental and health impacts as a result of the contamination of residents and surrounding areas (agriculture, water, ocean, communities, etc.), not to mention of the first responders, the SDF, U.S. personnel, government officials, and NGOs and NPOs working in the region. Second is the economic impact as a result of the evacuations, loss of livelihood of many people, and the unwillingness of others to buy exports (such as rice) from that region. Moreover, diplomatically and politically Japan has suffered as a result of the loss of trust in the government to handle the crisis in a forthright and transparent manner.

Today forty-eight of the fifty nuclear power reactors in Japan are shut down or suspended. A poll in June 2013 showed that while 46 percent of those surveyed were willing to see nuclear power reactors restarted if they were found to be structurally and seismically safe, almost 50 percent opposed the idea. Experts predict that the cost of electricity will rise 20–30 percent if the reactors remain down in the future. In order to cover the losses, consumers have been urged during the past couple of years to conserve where possible. The development of alternative forms of energy remains bureaucratically, legally, and technically slow. Politically, however, with the exception of the ruling Liberal Democratic Party, the other eight major parties all seek an end to Japan's reliance on nuclear power, which amounted to approximately 25 percent of Japan's energy production on the eve of March 11. More than any other issue, the messy intersection of vested interests, ideology, science, and national strategy can be seen here. It is no wonder that the people, as consumers, residents, workers, and voters of the earthquake and natural disaster country that Japan is, are confused. It is also no wonder that citizens of other countries, who will be impacted by Japan's decisions, are watching carefully.

It is certain that this problem will likely arise again in the future when another earthquake and tsunami hit. For this reason it is imperative that Japan make the right decisions as it prepares for its next megaquake and other disasters—whether they be volcanic, pandemic, or human (politico-socio-economic)—that follow.

Notes

TRANSLATOR'S FOREWORD

1. The Provincial Liaison Office's name has since changed to the Provincial Cooperation Office (Ōsaka Chihō Kyōryoku Honbu). There are fifty offices around the country, including four in Hokkaido Prefecture, and each one has subregional offices covering certain geographic or administrative areas. They are responsible for recruiting, managing retiree and reservist matters, and public affairs.

2. Robert D. Eldridge, "SDF-Student Workshops Prove Successful," *Daily Yomiuri*, January 1, 2002.

3. Takashima Tetsuo, *Kyodai jishin no hi: Inochi o mamoru tame no hontō no koto* (The day the large-scale earthquake comes to Japan: What we all truly need to know to preserve life) (Tokyo: Shueisha, 2006).

4. I had left Osaka University in late September 2009 to assume the position of deputy assistant chief of staff, G-5 (Community Policy, Planning, and Liaison), Marine Corps Bases Japan (now known as the G-7 [Government and External Affairs], Marine Corps Installations Pacific), and was working for the Marine Corps/Department of Defense at this point. The views in this book are my own and do not necessarily reflect those of the USMC, Department of Defense, or U.S. government.

5. Robert D. Eldridge and Alfred J. Woodfin, "Planning for the Inevitable: On the Need for Japan to Include U.S. Forces in the Response to a Large-Scale Disaster within the Country," *U.S.-Japan Alliance Affairs Series No. 5*, Center for International Security Studies and Policy, March 2006.

6. For the conference report, see Robert D. Eldridge and Murakami Tomoaki, *One Year after the Tsunami: Improving Civil-Military Relations in Disaster Assistance* (Toyonaka: Center for International Security Studies and Policy, 2006).

7. Eldridge and Woodfin, "Planning for the Inevitable." The Japanese version was Robert D. Eldridge and Alfred J. Woodfin, "Nihon ni okeru daikibo saigai kyūen katsudō to zainichi beigun no yakuwari ni tsuite no teigen," *Kokusai kōkyō seisaku kenkyū (International Public Policy Studies)* 11, no. 1 (September 2006): 143–158.

8. For the conference report, see James L. Schoff and Marina Travayiakis, *In Times of Crisis: U.S.-Japan Civil-Military Disaster Relief Coordination* (Herndon VA: Potomac Books, 2009). This report followed another previous joint U.S.-Japan research project between IFPA and my former institution, OSIPP, on crisis management. See James L. Schoff, *Crisis Management in Japan and the United States: Creating Opportunities for Cooperation amid Dramatic Change* (Dulles VA: Brassey's, 2004).

9. I even offered to sell my house in Hyogo Prefecture to him if he had so much confidence in Japan's ability (or any country's, for that matter) to respond on its own. (He did not take me up on the offer.) In November 2011, when I was a speaker at a conference on the role of the military in disasters sponsored by the Tokyo-based National Institute for Defense Studies (Bōei Kenkyūsho), I ran into one of the Japanese participants, who works for the United Nations and who had participated in that conference. She said the Japanese participants still talk about that heated exchange between me and the USAID official in 2006.

10. Email (Facebook message) from Takashima Tetsuo to Robert D. Eldridge, April 11, 2011.

11. Lieutenant General Glueck's quote can be found in the seventeen-minute video *Marine Corps Bases Japan-Hosted Home Stay Program, August 6–9, 2011, Camp Foster, Okinawa, Japan*, available at http://www.youtube.com/watch?v=q10m9Ii4lOYw; accessed January 2012.

12. Http://www.youtube.com/watch?v=q10m9Ii4lOYw; accessed January 2012.

13. For one of the best books about the Great Kanto Earthquake in English, see Joshua Hammer, *Yokohama Burning: The Deadly 1923 Earthquake and Fire That Helped Forge the Path to World War* (New York: Free Press, 2006).

14. One such talk took place a year after the disaster, on March 9, 2012, in Tokyo before an association of lawyers, politicians, and company presidents. The organizer and one of those in attendance played key roles on the Japanese side behind the scenes, significantly helping the U.S. side in its support of Japan. For this reason, the meeting, two days before the one-year anniversary of the disaster, was a particularly special setting.

15. For more on these observations, see Hiroe Jirō, Robert D. Eldridge, and Katsumata Hidemichi, "Behind the Scenes of Operation Tomodachi," *Japan Echo Web*, no. 8 (October–November 2011); http://www.japanechoweb.jp/diplomacy-politics/jew0801; accessed February 2012.

16. The official name of the conference, attended by close to six hundred Japanese SDF and Ministry of Defense (Bōeishō) civilian personnel, was "Presentations of Lessons Learned from the Great East Japan Earthquake" (Higashi Nihon daishinsai kyōkun seika happyōkai).

17. Takashima Tetsuo, *M8* (Tokyo: Shueisha, 2004); Takashima Tetsuo, *TSU-NAMI* (Tokyo: Shueisha, 2005); and Takashima, *Kyodai jishin no hi.*

18. See, for example, "Marines, Shizuoka Prefecture, Discuss Disaster Mitigation," *Okinawa Marine*, November 23, 2011; http://www.marines.mil /unit/mcbjapan/Documents/OkiMar/111123.pdf; accessed same date.

19. For more on Oshima, known as the "Green Pearl" for its pre-earthquake and tsunami beauty, see Robert D. Eldridge, "A Small Island's Big Lessons," *Daily Yomiuri*, June 30, 2011. For more on the homestay program, see the video at http://www.youtube.com/watch?v=q10m9I4lOYw (accessed March 11, 2012).

20. For more on these efforts, see Robert D. Eldridge, "After Operation Tomodachi, Relationships and Preparations Continue," *Japan Journal*, March 2012:26–28.

INTRODUCTION

1. Takashima, *M8*, 99.

2. Takashima, *M8*, 3.

3. A little more than a year after the original version of this book came out, a second earthquake struck the Niigata area in July 2007; it was called the Chuetsu Offshore Earthquake (Niigataken Chūetsu Oki Jishin).

4. Scholars and experts have offered different estimates about the magnitude of the earthquake. They have estimated it as between 8.8 and 9.3.

5. Takashima, *TSUNAMI*, 300, 334.

6. In fact, as readers know, Japan would subsequently experience a large-scale earthquake and tsunami during the Great East Japan Earthquake, an M9 megaquake that struck on March 11, 2011.

7. Takashima, *M8*, 197.

8. Takashima, *TSUNAMI*, 284, 303.

1. A MEGAQUAKE IN TOKYO

1. The ERC was one of two committees, the second being the Policy Committee (Seisaku Iinkai), making up the Headquarters for Earthquake Research Promotion (Jishin Chōsa Kenkyū Suishin Honbu). The Headquarters was established in accordance with the July 1995 Special Measure Law on Earthquake Disaster Prevention (Jishin Bōsai Taisaku Tokubetsu Sōchihō). It originally was attached to the Prime Minister's Office (Sōrifu) and now belongs to the Ministry of Education, Culture, Sports, Science, and Technology (Monbukagakushō).

2. Like some of the English names provided in this book, there is no official English name for the Tōkyō Bōsai Kaigi (confirmed in telephone interview by translator on February 23, 2012). This raises a concern because one

wonders how much Japan's disaster estimates are shared with non-Japanese organizations and whether Japanese organizations and agencies are able to adequately communicate with their international counterparts when even their organizations' names have not been provided in English.

3. The Japanese intensity scale is divided into ten levels: 0, 1, 2, 3, 4, 5-weak, 5-strong, 6-weak, 6-strong, and 7. For more on the Japanese seismic scale, otherwise known as *shindo*, see http://en.wikipedia.org/wiki/Japan_Meteorological_Agency_seismic_intensity_scale.

4. Ghastly photos of the victims of the firestorms show blackened bodies across a wide area. The area, located in present-day Sumida Ward (Sumida-ku), Tokyo, had been recently purchased by the Tokyo City Government (Tōkyō-shi) and was being converted to a park when the disaster hit. It is currently known as Yokoamicho Park (Yokoamichō Kōen) and houses a memorial (Tōkyōto Ireidō) to the victims of the Great Kanto Earthquake and the Tokyo air raids during World War II, as well as a museum (Fukkō Kinenkan).

5. A recent report produced by a government project team for the Japan Meteorological Agency (comprised primarily of researchers from the University of Tokyo's Earthquake Research Institute [Tōkyō Daigaku Jishin Kenkyūsho]) found that a future earthquake could register an intensity level 7, rather than a 6-strong, as previously thought. See "North Tokyo Bay Big One Could Top the Scale: Study," *Japan Times*, February 22, 2012; http://www.japantimes.co.jp/text/nn20120222a6.html; accessed same date.

6. The current dollar-yen conversion rate is $1.00 = 100 yen, and that rate is used in the figures cited in the volume.

7. The committee was established in August 2003 to review what had been done since the 1995 earthquake and summarize those findings by 2005, the tenth anniversary of the disaster. See "Fukkō 10 Nen Iinkai ga hossoku 5 nen 1 gatsu ni muke sōtenken" (Ten-year reconstruction committee established, review to be completed by January 2005), *Kōbe shimbun*, August 29, 2003. This committee is not to be confused with the Reconstruction Design Council (Fukkō Kōsō Kaigi), established on April 11, 2011, and discussed in the epilogue.

8. New studies suggest that following the March 11, 2011, earthquake, there has been pressure on the tectonic plates beneath Tokyo that has resulted in some changes, including the chance that two or more focal areas might end up moving simultaneously. See "Chances of Big Quake below Tokyo Rising," *Daily Yomiuri*, August 30, 2011.

9. One could add the subways to this list. See "Tokyo Faces Aging Infrastructure," *Japan News*, June 18, 2013.

10. A derailment near Amagasaki City on the JR Fukuchiyama Line caused the deaths of 106 morning commuters (and injured 562) when it crashed into an apartment building along a curve in April 2005.

11. Since this book was originally written in 2006, it was necessary to follow up to see about the status of the construction. JR East announced in May 2008 that the construction work was in fact completed. See the following press release (in Japanese) with two pages of before and after photos: http://www.jreast.co.jp/press/2008/20080503.pdf; accessed March 1, 2011. (The date for the link says May 3, but the press release itself is dated May 13.)

12. See "Shutokō ni notteiru toki, moshimo daijishin ga okitara dō sureba ii no ka (What are we supposed to do when we are driving on the Tokyo Metropolitan Expressway and are suddenly hit by an earthquake?); http://www.shutoko.jp/inquiry/qa/disaster.html#q1 (accessed February 23, 2012).

13. Eleven people, including 8 children, were crushed to death and almost 250 injured at a fireworks festival when panic ensued in a pedestrian overpass at Asagiri Station in Akashi City, west of Kobe, in July 2001.

14. Joshua Hammer's *Yokohama Burning* is one of the best books in English on the devastation wreaked by the fires.

15. See the website entitled "Disaster Prevention Information" at http://www.bousai.metro.tokyo.jp/japanese/knowledge/material_z.html (accessed February 25, 2012).

16. See http://www.bousai.metro.tokyo.jp/japanese/knowledge/material_z.html.

17. "Wagaya no ekijōka taisaku," the title of the document in Japanese, can be found at http://www.city.yokohama.lg.jp/shobo/kikikanri/ekijouka-map/ (accessed February 25, 2012).

18. Takahashi Manabu, "Tochi no rireki to Hanshin Daishinsai" (The record of the land and the Great Hanshin Earthquake), *Chirigaku hyōron* (Geography review), Series A, 69(7) (1996): 504–517.

19. Toda's paper can be found at http://www.aist.go.jp/aist_j/new_research/nr 20050610/nr20050610.html (accessed February 25, 2012).

20. See http://www.aist.go.jp/aist_j/new_research/nr20050610/nr20050610.html.

21. The East Chiba Prefecture Earthquake killed 2 people and injured more than 160.

22. See http://www.aist.go.jp/aist_j/new_research/nr20050610/nr20050610.html.

23. According to figures from the Ministry of Justice dated February 22, 2012, the number of registered non-Japanese citizens in Japan as of December

31, 2011, was 2,078,840, down for the third straight year in a row. In 2011, 55,671 foreigners left Japan, due in large part to the disaster and fears of nuclear contamination. This represented a 2.6 percent drop from the previous year's foreign population. See http://www.moj.go.jp/nyuukokukanri /kouhou/nyuukokukanri04_00015.html; accessed March 10, 2012.

24. Sadly there were numerous incidents after the March 11 disaster as well, including ATM thefts, at least one confirmed rape, and a case where a member of the GSDF stole money from the belongings of a body he had recovered. Some of the types of crimes to expect are discussed in greater detail in chapter 2.

25. Translator's note: I saw this in many settings, especially when our seminar at Kobe University, which was comprised of primarily Japanese and American undergraduate and graduate students, came together to do volunteer work in the affected area, despite many of the students being victims themselves.

26. Translator's note: This was equally true in the March 11, 2011, Great East Japan Earthquake, particularly when tens of thousands of U.S. military and government personnel and relief workers from around the world came to help in the affected area.

2. PROBLEMS FOLLOWING A MEGAQUAKE

1. "Indoyō Ōtsunami: Akka suru eisei jōtai" (The Indian Ocean tsunami and the worsening sanitary situation), *Sankei Shimbun*, January 6, 2005. According to an interview with the editor of the *Sankei Shimbun*, Nakashizu Keiichiro, the *Sankei* sent reporters from Singapore and Tokyo to cover the disaster. Email from Nakashizu Keiichirō to Robert D. Eldridge, February 7, 2012.

2. "Indoyō Ōtsunami."

3. "3,000 itai yukiba naku anchisho yorisoro izoku hitsugi fusoku; 'semete hayaku sogi'" (There is no place for 3,000 bodies; 'at least hold a funeral'), *Yomiuri Shimbun*, January 19, 1995. I wish to thank Mr. Saitō Osamu, senior research fellow, Editorial and Research Office of the Osaka headquarters of the *Yomiuri Shimbun*, for assistance with gathering past articles of the newspaper.

4. In light of the government of Japan's study in August 2012 announcing that there may be as many as 326,000 deaths in a triple Tokai, Tonankai, and Nankai earthquake scenario, it is hoped that Japanese authorities have many more body bags ready today. For more on this report, see the final chapter of this book.

5. "Setsushi saigai ni sonae DNA hozon" (Setsu City preparing for disasters by preserving DNA), *Sankei Shimbun*, August 16, 2005.

6. "Gareki shobun Amagasakioki de kuni to Kyōgi Hyōgoken Kasumigaseki Biru 20 to bun" (Hyogo Prefecture in discussions with central government over disposal of rubble in offshore Amagasaki, about 20 times the size of Kasumigaseki Building), *Yomiuri Shimbun*, January 26, 1995.

7. "Gareki shobun Amagasakioki de kuni to Kyōgi Hyōgoken Kasumigaseki Biru 20 to bun."

8. Translator's note: This is one of the primary reasons we—the Marine Corps and the U.S. Air Force Special Operations—focused first on getting the runway cleared at Sendai Airport in Miyagi Prefecture. We conducted our first meeting with airport authorities on the morning of March 15. At the time there were still hundreds of vehicles and debris on the runway itself, but by the end of the week, U.S. military aircraft began landing at the airport. One month later civilian operations had been partially restored with charter flights. Initially Japanese government and airport officials expressed doubt their partially submerged airfield could be restored as quickly as it was, but they supported our efforts. Mr. Azuma Shōzō, then senior vice minister for disaster management, played a critical role in helping to coordinate the recovery of Sendai Airport in the initial days.

9. "Zenhankaiya no kaitai kōhi de zengaku futan kojin jutaku manshon taisho seifu kettei gareki jōkyō isogu" (Central government to cover costs of demolishing destroyed homes; private homes and apartments covered as well; government hurries to decide on removal of debris), *Yomiuri Shimbun*, January 29, 1995.

10. "Indoyō Ōtsunami."

11. "Hisaiten arashi 20 ken Sannomiya, Motomachi higai ichiokuen kikinzoku, Ōsaka de kankin" (20 stores in disaster area robbed; losses of 100 million yen in Sannomiya and Motomachi; gold sold in Osaka), *Yomiuri Shimbun*, February 10, 1995.

12. "Akushitsu shinsai shōhō ga yokugyō 'Shi kara haken' hōgai na shurihi yōkyu (Illegal charge for repairs, saying "The city sent us"), *Yomiuri Shimbun*, February 4, 1995.

13. "Yoshin dema ni madowasarenaide fukuramu fuan hitoriaruki guraa to kitemo reisei Kōdō o Hanshin-Awaji Daishinsaigo yoshin no fuan karaka, oku no dema jōhō ga tonda" (People not being misled by rumors about aftershocks; anxiety spreads and takes on a life of its own; behave calmly even if an earthquake comes; after the Great Hanshin-Awaji Earthquake much false information circulated, probably from fear of aftershocks), *Yomiuri Shimbun*, January 26, 1995. The Interfaculty Initiative in Information Studies merged with two other institutions at Tokyo University, the Earthquake Research Institute and the Institute of Industrial Science, to form the Center for Integrated Disaster Information Research (CIDIR;

Jōhō Gakkan Sōgō Bōsai Jōhō Kenkyū Sentaa) in 2008. Hiroi, who passed away in April 2006, donated his collection of materials, which forms the basis of the CIDIR's archives.

14. "Yoshin dema ni madowasarenaide."

15. "Hisai shōmei no hakkō uchikiri dema nagare shimin sattō" (Residents crowd [city offices] amid rumors about discontinuance of issuing of disaster identification certificates), *Yomiuri Shimbun*, February 8, 1995.

16. "Gienkin sagi nado bōshi ni zenryoku Keisatsuchō (Full cooperation necessary in preventing fraud in relief donations to National Police Agency)," *Yomiuri Shimbun*, February 4, 1995.

17. For a flier that was handed out at the time warning people early on of potentially illicit organizations, see http://www.ss-igari.com/image/B5C1D9 D0B6E2BABEB5BDA1A1C3EDB0D5B4ADB5AFA5C1A5E9A5B7.pdf#se arch='%E7%BE%A9%E6%8D%90%E9%87%91+%E8%A9%90%E6% AC%BA+%E6%96%B0%E6%BD%9F%E4%B8%AD%E8%B6%8A%E5 %9C%B0%E9%9C%87'.

18. The email appeared on the following blog: http://blog.livedoor.jp/taroatwork /archives/8605510.html.

3. TRENCH-TYPE MEGAQUAKES

1. Shōwa is the Japanese name for the period during which Emperor Hirohito reigned—namely, 1925–1989. Nankai, as we saw above, literally means "South Seas" and denotes an earthquake scenario for the offshore area from Wakayama Prefecture down to Kyushu.

2. The Japanese people are historically superstitious about earthquakes and tsunamis, relating them to events that have recently happened. One wonders, therefore, if some people in Japan at the time drew a linkage between the December 7, 1944, Tonankai Earthquake and the December 7, 1941, attacks on Pearl Harbor, thinking that the earthquake might have been revenge for an ill-fated adventure.

3. In 2012 this number was greatly revamped, as discussed in the last chapter.

4. On this theme see Edan Corkill, "Danger Zones," *Japan Times*, February 26, 2012.

5. In April 2012 a joint project among Kansai University (Kansai Daigaku); the Ministry of Land, Infrastructure, Transport, and Tourism; and the Ministry of Internal Affairs and Communications began to study tsunami heights and speeds using an ocean wave observation radar system normally used to monitor tidal currents. See "Wave Radar May Help Tsunami Predictions," *Daily Yomiuri*, March 14, 2012.

6. Dr. Funabashi Yōichi, then the chief editor of the *Asahi Shimbun*, has written, "Throughout Japanese history, seismic disasters have often seemed

to mark the dramatic end of an era. Closely following Commodore Matthew Perry's conclusion of a trade treaty in 1854 came the Ansei Great Earthquakes of 1854 and 1855; the Great Kanto Earthquake of 1923 struck shortly after the annulment of the Anglo-Japanese Alliance in 1922; the advent of Japan's lost era coincided with the Great Hanshin Earthquake in 1995. The momentous question now is what sort of change the Great Eastern Japan Earthquake will delineate." See Yoichi Funabashi, "March 11—Japan's Zero Hour," in *Reimagining Japan: The Quest for a Future That Works*, ed. McKinsey and Company (San Francisco: Viz Media, 2011), 8. Funabashi, who served as the program director of the Independent Investigation Commission on the Fukushima Daiichi Nuclear Accident, which was established in September 2011 to independently examine the Fukushima disaster, established the (Rebuild Japan Initiative Foundation (Ippan Zaidan Hōjin Nihon Saiken Inishiachibu) in March 2011 shortly after the disaster and is now its chairman. In early 2013 he published a book in Japanese about the nuclear disaster at Fukushima and is currently working on an updated version to be published in English. See Funabashi Yōichi, *Merutodaun-Kauntodaun* (Meltdown-countdown) (Tokyo: Bungei Shunju, 2013).

7. It is worrisome that Japanese officials tend to underestimate the number of deaths in a major disaster. This tendency was confirmed in two separate interviews with Tokyo Metropolitan Government officials and central government (Cabinet) officials. See Eldridge and Woodfin, "Planning for the Inevitable."

8. Some scholars think these estimates are low. See Eldridge and Woodfin, "Planning for the Inevitable," for the views of those authors as well as those of some of the experts cited.

9. The original Japanese title of the document is "Tōkai jishin no yochi to bōsai taiō: 'Tōkai jishin ni kansuru jōhō' o tadashiku katsuyō shite itadaku tame ni" (Tokyo: Central Disaster Management Council, 2003).

10. "Genpatsu shinsai, yomenu higai tōkai jishin, sono toki hamaoka (Nuclear disaster: It is impossible to tell what will happen at Hamaoka [nuclear power plan] in a Tokai earthquake)," *Asahi Shimbun*, October 13, 2004. Koide, who has been a strong critic of the Japanese government's nuclear policies, is being listened to more and more, to the extent that some in the government are reported as wanting to "'drag someone like Koide' into the process of drawing up the government's new energy policy." See "Japan Political Pulse: Fumbling Government Faces Huge Challenges in 2012," *Mainichi Daily News*, December 26, 2011; http://mdn.mainichi.jp/perspectives/pulse/news/20111226p2a00m0na002000c.html (accessed February 29, 2012).

11. For more on the 1981 guidelines and the subsequent efforts at revising them prior to the March 11, 2011, disaster, see the special edition of the journal of the Japan Association for Earthquake Engineering (*Nihon Jishin Kōgaku Kaishi*), No. 5 (January 2007): 1–53, at http://www.jaee.gr.jp /jp/wp-content/uploads/2012/02/kaishi05.pdf#search='%E7%99%BA %E9%9B%BB%E7%94%A8%E5%8E%9F%E5%AD%90%E6%88%B8%E 6%96%BD%E8%A8%AD%E3%81%AB%E9%96%A2%E3%81%99%E3% 82%8B%E8%80%90%E9%9C%87%E8%A8%AD%E8%A8%88%E5%AF %A9%E6%9F%BB%E6%8C%87%E9%87%9D+1981'.

4. TSUNAMIS

1. The predecessor to the PTWC was the Tsunami Warning Center, established by the U.S. government at Ewa Beach, Oahu, following the 1946 earthquake and tsunami in the Aleutian Islands that damaged Hawaii as well.

2. Minoru Matsutani, "Nankai Quake Projected Toll Radically Raised: 3/11 Realities Point to 300,000-plus Deaths, Vast Tsunami Devastation," *Japan Times*, August 30, 2012.

3. Matsutani, "Nankai Quake Projected Toll Radically Raised."

4. Readers may remember images from Kesennuma City, Miyagi Prefecture, where twenty-two fuel tanks leaked fuel into the bay, which eventually became a "sea of fire" in the March 11 disaster, burning over the next couple of days.

5. In fact a magnitude 9 earthquake occurred in 2011 off the coast of Miyagi Prefecture. Iwate, just to the north, was heavily damaged as well.

6. Katada Toshitaka, Kuwasawa Noriyuki, Kanai Masanobu, and Hosoi Kyohei, "Tsunami hinan no ishikettei kōzō ni kansuru kenkyū" (Research on decision making when taking refuge from a tsunami), available at http:// dsel.ce.gunma-u.ac.jp/doc/n089.pdf#search='%E4%B8%89%E9%87% 8D%E7%9C%8C%E5%B0%BE%E9%B7%B2%E5%B8%82%E5%9C%B0 %E9%9C%87++%E7%BE%A4%E9%A6%AC%E5%A4%A7%E5%AD%A 6+2004%E5%B9%B49%E6%9C%88'.

For more on this study and others, see the website of the Disaster Social Engineering Lab (Saigai Shakai Kōgaku Kenkyūshitsu) of Gunma University at http://dsel.ce.gunma-u.ac.jp/ (accessed June 2014).

7. Quoted in "Chuō Bōsai Kaigi Kyōiku-Kyōkun Hanshin-Awaji Chōsa" (Central Disaster Management Council report on education and lessons learned from Hanshin-Awaji Earthquake); http://www.bousai.go.jp/kyoiku/kyokun /hanshin_awaji/chosa/pdf/169.pdf (accessed June 18, 2014), 5.

8. This situation occurred the night of the March 11, 2011, earthquake, and many commuters in the Tokyo area had to walk home or wait for buses.

9. Kobe Airport, opened in 2007, after this book was completed, is built on landfill and could be impacted by a tsunami. For more on Kobe Airport, see Robert D. Eldridge and Alfred J. Woodfin, "Marine Air: The Opening of Kōbe Airport and Considerations for Military Pilots," *U.S.-Japan Alliance Affairs Series No. 4*, Center for International Security Studies and Policy, March 2006.

10. Road damage was very visible in the Tohoku disaster of March 11, 2011.

11. On operations from the sea, see Wallace C. Gregson, James North, and Robert D. Eldridge, "Responses to Humanitarian Assistance and Disaster Relief: A Future Vision for U.S.-Japan Combined Sea-Based Deployment," *International Public Policy Studies* (Kokusai kōkyō seisaku kenkyū) 12, no. 2 (March 2008): 37–47. This is the English version of an article prepared in 2004 and published in three installments between April and June 2005 in the journal *Securitarian*, published by the (Japan Defense Agency (Bōeichō), now the Ministry of Defense (Bōeishō).

12. "Tsunami shisha sōtei no bai ijō? Tōnankai-Nankai jishin 'Indoyō' no hakairyoku chūmoku Naikakufu minaoshi (Will the expected death toll from a tsunami be twice as high? Reevaluation by the Cabinet Office of the Tonankai and Nankai earthquakes after witnessing the destructive power of the Indian Ocean Earthquake)," *Sankei Shimbun*, June 6, 2006.

5. DISASTER PREVENTION AND REDUCTION

1. See Chūō Bōsai Kaigi, "Minami Kantō chiiki chokka no jishin taisaku ni kansuru taikō" (Guidelines for disaster measures in a direct hit earthquake in the southern Kanto area); http://www.bousai.go.jp/shinsai/principles/body0.html (accessed February 6, 2012).

2. Camp Tachikawa hosts, among other units, the headquarters of the Eastern Army Aviation Group (Tōbu Hōmen Kōkutai).

3. "'Hanshin daishinsai kara 10 nen keikaku' 2 miyako, shodo taisei no jūjitsu o isogu" (10 years after the great Hanshin disaster, 2: It is necessary to speed up the capital's early response system), *Sankei Shimbun*, January 14, 2005.

4. *Defense of Japan 2001* (Tokyo: Urban Connections, 2001), 198. According to a footnote in the white paper, other officials include the director general of the Japan Coast Guard (Kaijō Hoanchō Chōkan), chief of the Regional Maritime Safety Headquarters (Kanku Kaijō Hoan Honbuchō), and general managers of airports.

5. For more on the concept of sea operations and their applicability to Japan, see Gregson, North, and Eldridge, "Responses to Humanitarian Assistance and Disaster Relief."

6. At the time of the December 2004 disaster, the translator was serving on the staff of Marine Forces Pacific (MFP) in Hawaii. Immediately following a meeting with the senior leadership on December 26 with representatives of the Honolulu-based Center of Excellence in Disaster Management and Humanitarian Assistance, notes of the meeting—namely, items that Japan would theoretically be able to provide if it so desired to support the international relief effort that would likely form—were shared with the Japanese liaison officer of the Joint Staff Office, whose office was near mine, with the permission of the commanding general of MFP. This information was forwarded to Ichigaya, the contemporary headquarters of the Self-Defense Forces. It is uncertain, therefore, why it took the SDF almost five weeks to fully begin their relief operations.

7. Yomiuri Shimbunsha, ed., *Yomiuri hōdō shashin Hanshin daishinsai zenkiroku* (Yomiuri photographic reporting: Complete records of the Hanshin earthquake) (Tokyo: Yomiuri Shimbun, 1995). All quotes in the timeline are from this volume.

8. "TKC to Shizuoka Ken Kanbarachō, Tōkai jishin o sōtei shi, netto keiyu no deeta fukkyu o kenshō (TKC and Kanbara Town, Shizuoka Prefecture, examine restoring data through Internet in the event of a Tokai earthquake)"; http://japan.internet.com/public/news/20041224/5.html (accessed February 6, 2012).

9. Ironically many data were found to be lost from the Social Insurance Agency in 2007 after the agency had attempted to merge its computerized systems in 1997. Due to numerous scandals and the loss of information on tens of millions of pension holders, the agency, which had been under the Ministry of Health, Welfare, and Labor, was dissolved on December 31, 2009, and reorganized as the Japan Pension Service (Nihon Nenkin Kikō). It remains under the same ministry, however.

10. "KDDI ga eisei keitai denwa 'Irijium,' 5 nen buri ni kokunai fukkatsu" (KDDI is reintroducing satellite phone "Iridium" for first time in five years); http://itpro.nikkeibp.co.jp/free/ncc/news/20050601/161969/ (accessed March 6, 2012).

6. WHAT JAPAN IS DOING AND SHOULD DO

1. The Coordination Committee of Earthquake Prediction Research is now known as the Coordination Committee of Earthquake and Volcanic Eruption Prediction Researches (Jishin Kazan Funka Yochi Kenkyū Kyōgikai), following the merger in May 2006 of the earthquake council with the Coordination Committee of Volcanic Eruption Prediction Research (Kazan Funka Yochi Kenkyū Kyōgikai). I would like to thank Mr. Miura Satoshi

and Mr. Morita Yuichi of the committee for providing me with the official English name of the group by e-mail correspondence.

2. This law went into effect in November 1959, following the Ise Bay typhoon that struck on September 26, wreaking havoc on the Kii Peninsula (Wakayama and Mie Prefectures) and nearby Gifu and Aichi Prefectures and killing approximately five thousand people. Articles 11–13 of the law cover the establishment and organization of the Central Disaster Management Council.

3. This law was first passed in July 1995 and has subsequently been revised.

4. The institute is now known as the Geospatial Information Authority of Japan.

5. The ERI was established in 1925, following the Great Kanto Earthquake of September 1923.

6. The institute was originally established in April 1963 as the National Research Center for Earth Science and Disaster Prevention (Kokuritsu Bōsai Kagaku Kenkyū Sentaa) under the Science and Technology Agency (Kagaku Gijutsuchō). It was scheduled to be merged with another organization, but that 2007 decision was later rescinded.

7. The agency was originally created as the Marine Science and Technology Center in 1971 upon the recommendations of the Japan Federation of Economic Organizations (Nihon Keizai Dantai Rengō, or Keidanren), now known as the Japan Business Federation. It was reorganized and renamed in 2004.

8. The institute was created in April 2001 as a result of the merger of fifteen separate think tanks and organizations, some tracing their history as far back as 1882. It has two headquarters, one in Tokyo and the other in Tsukuba City, and centers throughout the country.

9. The institute is now known as the National Institute of Information and Communications Technology (Jōhō Tsūshin Kenkyū Kikō), which was created by a merger of the CRL and the Telecommunications Advancement Organization (Tsūshin Hōsō Kikō) in April 2004.

10. This report was adopted by the General Assembly of the Geodesy Council with the launch of its first prediction plan in 1964.

11. For more on this earthquake, see K. Wang, "Predicting the 1975 Haicheng Earthquake," *Bulletin of the Seismological Society of America* 96, no. 3 (2006): 757–795; K. T. Wu et al., "Case 2 Foreshocks to the Haicheng Earthquake of 1975: Certain Characteristics of the Haicheng Earthquake (M=7.3) Sequence," in *Evaluation of Proposed Earthquake Precursors*, ed. Max Wyss (Washington DC: American Geophysical Union, 1991), 12–14; Zhonghao Shou, "The Haicheng Earthquake and Its Prediction," *Science and Utopya*

65 (1999): 34; http://www.earthquakesignals.com/zhonghao296/a010 720.html (accessed January 11, 2012); Maryann Mott, "Can Animals Sense Earthquakes?" *National Geographic News* (November 2003), at http://news .nationalgeographic.com/news/2003/11/1111_031111_earthquakeanimals .html (accessed January 11, 2012).

12. The Nojima Fault (Nojima Dansō) cuts across Awaji Island off of Hyogo Prefecture proper and is a branch of the Japan Median Tectonic Line, which runs the length of the southern half of the main island of Honshu.

13. As an example, see Nagamatsu Shingo, *Gensai seisaku nyūmon: Kyōdai saigai risuku no gabanansu to shijō keizai* (An introduction to disaster mitigation policy: The governance of large-scale disaster risks and the market economy) (Tokyo: Kobun, 2008).

14. The prime minister at the time was Murayama Tomiichi, the chairman of the Social Democratic Party of Japan who headed a coalition government with the once long-ruling Liberal Democratic Party of Japan. In addition to problems with his leadership style, for which he was criticized by the people of the disaster area, there were also numerous structural and other problems in the political world and bureaucracy that had not been seriously addressed before that time.

15. The Northridge Earthquake occurred at 4:31 a.m., Pacific Standard Time, or 7:31 Eastern Standard Time.

16. "FEMA's Mission," cited on FEMA website, www.fema.gov/about/index .shtm (accessed January 23, 2012).

CONCLUSION

1. Takashima, as one of the first people interviewed following the March 11 disaster, called on readers to "keep it in mind that Japan is an earthquake-prone nation" and suggested that "videos and newspaper articles reporting the devastation caused by the latest quake should be kept and viewed repeatedly in the coming years." See Tetsuo Takashima, "Point of View: Support around-the-Clock Work to Prevent Nuclear Catastrophe," *Asahi Shimbun*, March 17, 2011; http://ajw.asahi.com/article/0311disaster/fukushima /aj201103173022 (accessed April 12, 2011).

EPILOGUE

1. Takashima, *Tsunami*.

2. "Learn the Lessons of Earthquakes, for Big Ones Will Happen Again," *Daily Yomiuri*, January 17, 2012.

3. Eldridge continues to write extensively on this issue and travels around Japan promoting closer relations between local communities and the U.S. Marine Corps in disaster cooperation; he defines such relations as

discussing mutual capabilities and concerns while getting to know one another, building trust and face-to-face relationships, before a disaster.

4. The Study Group's work can be found on the Cabinet Office's website at http://www.bousai.go.jp/jishin/nankai/model/ (accessed March 2013).

5. Nankai Torafu no Kyodai Jishin Moderu Kentō Iinkai, ed., *Nankai Torafu no kyodai jishin ni yoru shindo bunpu-tsunamidaka ni tsuite (daiichiji hōkoku)* (First report on the location of seismic activity and tsunami heights as a result of a Nankai Trough megaquake) (Tokyo: Naikakufu, 2013); available at http://www.bousai.go.jp/jishin/nankai/model/pdf/1st_report.pdf.

6. Minoru Matsutani, "Nankai Quake Projected Toll Radically Raised: 3/11 Realities Point to 300,000-plus Deaths, Vast Tsunami Devastation," *Japan Times*, August 30, 2012. For the actual report see Nankai Torafu no Kyodai Jishin Moderu Kentō Iinkai, ed., *Tsunami danso moderu hen: Tsunami danso moderu to tsunamidaka-shinsuiikito ni tsuite (daini hōkoku)* (Second report, tsunami fault model edition: Tsunami fault model and tsunami height and inundation areas) (Tokyo: Naikakufu, 2013); available at http://www.bousai.go.jp/jishin/nankai/model/pdf/20120829_2nd_report01.pdf.

7. Tokyo: Futabasha, 2011. Like many foreigners in Japan, Geller sometimes feels like a lone voice in the wind. See his interview, which took the form of an article, in Robaato Geraa, "'Sōteigai' to iu sanbun shibai" (Earthquake prediction is impossible: Avoiding responsibility by claiming [3.11 was] "unexpected"), *Chūō Kōron* 126, no. 7 (July 2011): 104–112.

8. Tokyo: Besutoseraazu, 2011.

9. Cited in Rob Gilhooly, "The Future of Earthquake Prediction? Skeptics Abound but Professor Claims Breakthrough in Research," *Japan Times*, December 28, 2011.

10. The committee's report can be found at http://www.bousai.go.jp/kaigirep /chuobou/suishinkaigi/english/index.html (accessed June 2013).

11. The Working Group's studies can be found on the Cabinet Office's website at http://www.bousai.go.jp/jishin/nankai/taisaku_wg/index.html (accessed June 2013).

12. The council's activities can be found on the Cabinet Office's website at http://www.bousai.go.jp/jishin/nankai/taisaku/index.html (accessed June 2013).

13. Cited in Shimazaki Kunihiko and Yanagida Kunio, "Higashi Nihon daishinsai sannenme no kyōkun: Jishin yochi to genpatsu no 'zenshinsō'" (Lessons from the Great East Japan Earthquake in the third year since the disaster: The "depths" of earthquake prediction and the nuclear power plants), *Bungei Shunjū* 91, no. 4 (April 2013): 305.

14. See "Report of the Committee for Technical Investigation on Counter-measures for Earthquakes and Tsunamis Based on the Lessons Learned

from the '2011 off the Pacific Coast of Tohoku Earthquake,'" at http://www.bousai.go.jp/kaigirep/chousakai/tohokukyokun/pdf/Report.pdf (accessed June 2013).

15. Cited in Shimazaki and Yanagida, "Higashi Nihon daishinsai sannenme no kyōkun," 303.

16. Cited in Shimazaki and Yanagida, "Higashi Nihon daishinsai sannenme no kyōkun," 306.

17. Noda Yoshihiko succeeded Kan, who had resigned, in September 2011. In December 2012 the ruling Minshutō (Democratic Party of Japan) lost badly in the general elections and Abe Shinzō, a former prime minister from the opposition Jiyū Minshutō (Liberal Democratic Party), took over.

18. Several books published by non-Japanese have addressed this debate. See McKinsey and Company, *Reimagining Japan*; Jeff Kingston, ed., *Natural Disaster and Nuclear Crisis in Japan: Response and Recovery after Japan's 3/11* (London: Routledge, 2012); and Richard J. Samuels, *3.11: Disaster and Change in Japan* (Ithaca NY: Cornell University Press, 2013).

19. See Gerald L. Curtis, "Tōhoku Diary: Reportage on the Tōhoku Disaster," in Kingston, *Natural Disaster and Nuclear Crisis in Japan*.

20. For Iokibe's comments see the video of his press conference at the Foreign Press Center in Tokyo on June 25, 2011, at http://video.search.yahoo.co.jp/search?ei=utf-8&fr=top_ga1_sa&p=Iio+%e6%bd%a4+%e6%95%99%e6%8e%88 (accessed June 2013).

21. Cited in "Grand Designs for Reconstruction," *Highlighting Japan*, September 2011; at http://www.gov-online.go.jp/eng/publicity/book/hlj/html/201109/201109_09.html (accessed June 2013).

22. Cited in "Grand Designs for Reconstruction."

23. The English version of the report is available at http://www.cas.go.jp/jp/fukkou/english/pdf/report20110625.pdf (accessed June 2013).

24. "Iokibe Gichō 'Fukkō, socchoku ni itte osoi'; Fukkō Kōsōkaigi ni sanji hosei nado hōkoku (Chairman Iokibe [says] "Honestly speaking, the reconstruction is too slow"; Reconstruction Design Council gets updated on third supplementary budget)," *Sankei Shimbun*, November 10, 2011.

25. Cited in Paul Blustein, "A Wakeup Call Japan Ignored," *Japan Times*, March 14, 2012.

26. The op-ed was reprinted in a Japan-based English-language newspaper. See Yoshihiko Noda, "Renew Commitment to Building a New Japan," *Japan Times*, March 14, 2012.

27. Iokibe Makoto, "Tōhoku no daichi ni 'fukko no tsuchioto' ga narihibiku toki" (The time when the "sounds of reconstruction" echo throughout the Tohoku region), *Chūō Kōron* 128, no. 4 (April 2013): 106–110.

28. Iokibe, "Tōhoku no daichi ni," 110.

Index